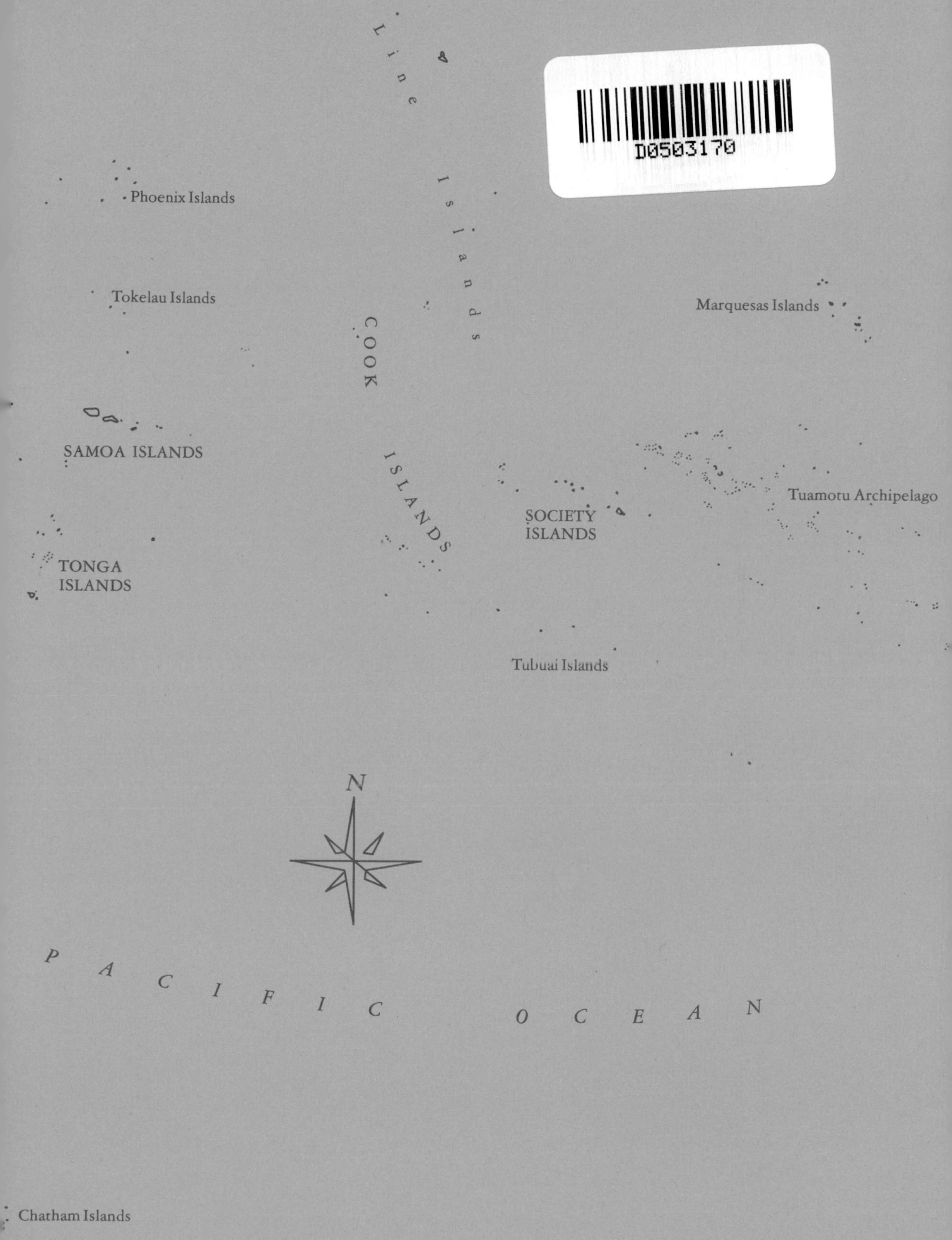

Line Islands

· Phoenix Islands

Tokelau Islands

Marquesas Islands

COOK

SAMOA ISLANDS

ISLANDS

Tuamotu Archipelago

SOCIETY
ISLANDS

TONGA
ISLANDS

Tubuai Islands

N

P A C I F I C   O C E A N

Chatham Islands

Cloth binding on this book reproduces in about half-size a design of Tonga tapa, feltlike material made from the inner bark of the paper mulberry tree and used for clothing and bedding. Stylized leis of leaves and seeds form this pattern.

Lesser bird of paradise (right), one of nearly 40 species that brighten New Guinea's dark forests, wears a snowy cascade of feathers more than a foot long.

Isles of the
SOUTH PAC

BY MAURICE SHADBOLT AND OLAF RUHEN

PREPARED BY THE SPECIAL PUBLICATIONS DIVISION,
Robert L. Breeden, Chief

NATIONAL GEOGRAPHIC SOCIETY, WASHINGTON, D.C.

Melvin M. Payne, President
Melville Bell Grosvenor, Editor-in-Chief
Gilbert M. Grosvenor, Editor

ISLES OF THE SOUTH PACIFIC
BY MAURICE SHADBOLT AND
OLAF RUHEN

Published by
THE NATIONAL GEOGRAPHIC SOCIETY
MELVIN M. PAYNE, *President*
MELVILLE BELL GROSVENOR,
    Editor-in-Chief
GILBERT M. GROSVENOR, *Editor*

Prepared by
THE SPECIAL PUBLICATIONS DIVISION

ROBERT L. BREEDEN, *Editor*
DONALD J. CRUMP, *Associate Editor*
PHILIP B. SILCOTT, *Manuscript Editor*
CYNTHIA RAMSAY, *Research*
TEE LOFTIN SNELL, BETTY STRAUSS,
    PEGGY WINSTON, *Research Assistants*
RONALD M. FISHER, MARY ANN
    HARRELL, TEE LOFTIN SNELL,
    GERALD S. SNYDER, *Picture Legends*
JOHANNA G. FARREN, *Style*
LUBA BALKO, MARGARET S. DEAN,
    CAROL OAKES, URSULA ROTH,
    BARBARA WALKER, *Staff Assistants*

Illustrations and Design
MICHAEL E. LONG, *Picture Editor*
JOSEPH A. TANEY, *Art Director*
JOSEPHINE B. BOLT, *Assistant Art
    Director*

Production and Printing
ROBERT W. MESSER, *Production*
JAMES R. WHITNEY, *Engraving and
    Printing*

DOROTHY CORSON, ANNE MCCAIN,
    Index

Revision Staff

MARY ANN HARRELL, *Manuscript
    Editor;* ANN H. CROUCH, *Research;*
    URSULA PERRIN, *Design Assistant;*
    JOHN R. METCALFE, *Engraving and
    Printing;* MARGARET MURIN
    SKEKEL, *Production Assistant;*
    RAJA D. MURSHED, JOAN PERRY,
    Staff Assistants

*Fogaʻafu Falls splashes over young Poly-
nesians on Western Samoa's Upolu Island. Overleaf: Canoeists fish by lantern
light as the sun dips behind the ragged
heights of Moorea, just west of Tahiti.*

DAVID MOORE, BLACK STAR (RIGHT), AND LUIS MARDEN,
NATIONAL GEOGRAPHIC STAFF (OVERLEAF)

Foreword

THE JET AGE really roared into my consciousness one Friday afternoon a few years ago. I excused myself from a meeting of the Board of Trustees of the National Geographic Society at exactly 5 p.m. in the center of Washington, D. C.

"Tomorrow morning I'm committed to join a scuba-diving expedition in Tahiti," I explained to my envious colleagues.

At 6 p.m. my wife Donna and I stepped aboard a westbound jet. By dawn we were talking with friendly Polynesians in Tahiti. And a little later—still well before noon—we crossed a narrow channel by boat to the island of Moorea. Before lunch we felt warm sand under our bare feet, and swam among brilliant coral reefs ringed by steep green peaks. Overnight we had flown to the heart of the South Pacific.

"How long can it last unspoiled?" Donna wondered. We saw some swift changes established and others rapidly approaching. Before many years pass, a good number of these timeless, languorous isles will wear a different face.

And the very fact of that transition is the reason for this book: to catch a vast but fleeting world before it changes. At no other moment in history has it been possible for a traveler to see such a sweep of time and space: outriggers like those used by the first island explorers, landfalls unchanged since the voyages of Captain Cook, the faces and costumes as Gauguin painted them, the beachcombing ease that represents escape to all of us in this hectic 20th century. Such a varied view has never been possible before—and the moment is highly perishable. The very technology that brings it close to us will soon transform it.

We still have time—however brief—to see these isles. For that reason, your Society commissioned two authors, both New Zealand-born, to cover the widespread subject: Maurice Shadbolt and Olaf Ruhen, longtime students of South Pacific isles and cultures. And thus this volume brings you a report that is broad, personal—and as timely as your library clock. With the special National Geographic map included with this book you island-hop with our authors—and with photographers David Moore and Jack Fields.

You will find surprises as I did. Could New Caledonia *really* have such modern buildings? And could Fiji—that newly independent, hotel-studded crossroad of the Pacific—still have areas so remote from the world's bustle and racket? For me, the words, maps, paintings, and photographs fill this book with surprises—and at least one surprise surrounds it: the authentic Tonga tapa design on the binding.

Some readers will find their discoveries mixing with memories: The horror of Guadalcanal in World War II is evoked by rust-enshrouded tanks and vine-covered shells. Yet the wartime strategy of island-hopping opened new routes and opportunities for the Solomons. Pacific veterans will be astonished at the change.

Mines, factories, bridges, and big new schools with brown-skinned rugby players—we see them all. Yet such progressive intrusions still cannot obscure the Stone Age aura, the colorful tabus, the names—Pago Pago, Bora Bora—that themselves sound like sea chanties.

Here, then, is the real-life romance of a world that still shimmers bright as a bubble. Enjoy it here—while you can.

Gilbert M. Grosvenor

Contents

Dazzling plumes and lengths of fur adorn a painted New Guinea Highlander; bird of paradise feathers and cassowary quills pierce his nose.

JACK FIELDS

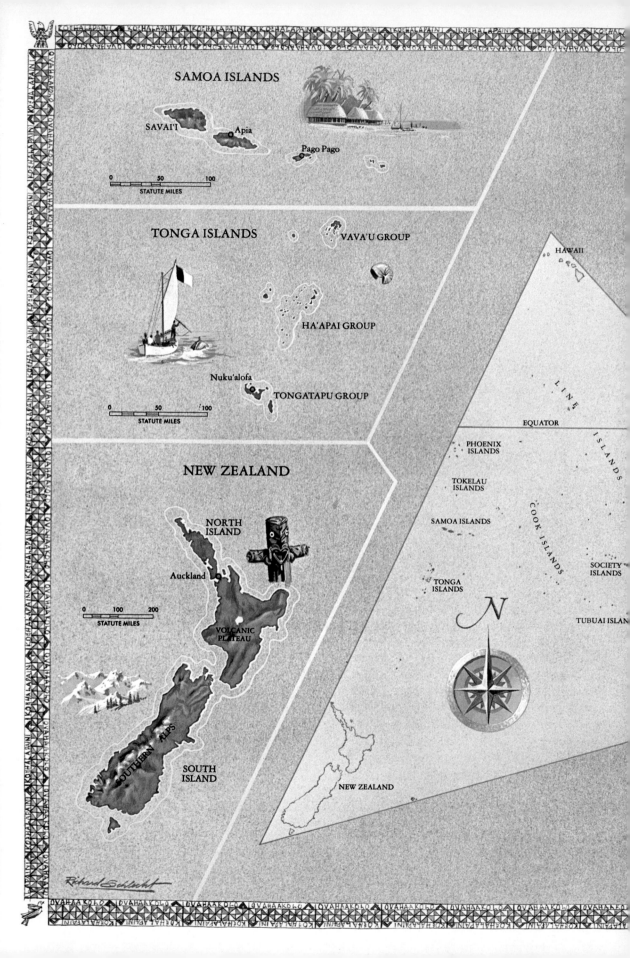

SAMOA ISLANDS

SAVAI'I

Apia

Pago Pago

0   50   100
STATUTE MILES

TONGA ISLANDS

VAVA'U GROUP

HA'APAI GROUP

Nuku'alofa

TONGATAPU GROUP

0   50   100
STATUTE MILES

NEW ZEALAND

NORTH
ISLAND

Auckland

0   100   200
STATUTE MILES

VOLCANIC
PLATEAU

SOUTHERN ALPS

SOUTH
ISLAND

HAWAII

LINE ISLANDS

EQUATOR

PHOENIX
ISLANDS

TOKELAU
ISLANDS

SAMOA ISLANDS

COOK ISLANDS

TONGA
ISLANDS

SOCIETY
ISLANDS

TUBUAI ISLAN

N

NEW ZEALAND

Richard Schlecht

P O L Y N E S I A

Polynesia—"many islands"—takes its shape from volcanic peaks and coral atolls, clear as a constellation among stars: a triangle defined by Hawaii above the Equator, New Zealand toward the southern ice, and Easter Island far to the east, pointing like a spear tip toward dawn. Through the centuries, a tall, brown-skinned people made this ocean realm their own. By accident or by design—authorities differ—the men of the long canoes found sun-washed islands by the hundred. The Polynesians' soft-flowing languages share words from a common stock to tell the myths of creation, the descent of chiefs from gods, the voyages of ancestral heroes, the welcome offered to travelers from other lands. Only in the day of jets do the vast distances of the Pacific yield to speed, and Maurice Shadbolt, who has written of Oceania for the NATIONAL GEOGRAPHIC, tells of Polynesian islands today —the life of those who call them home, the discoveries of those who visit.

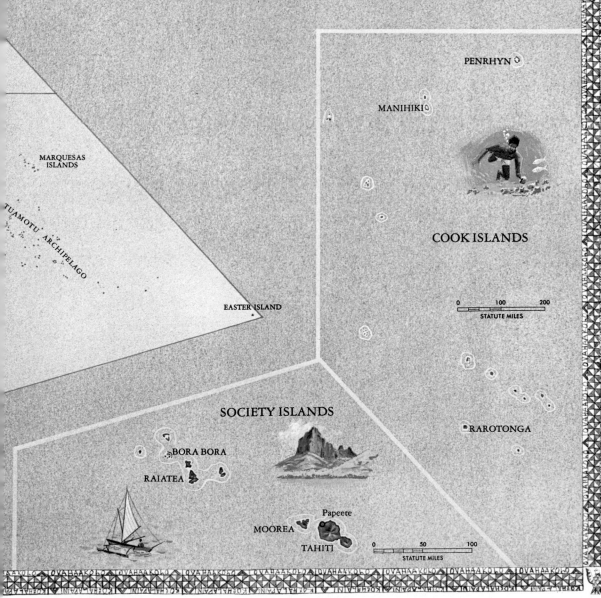

PENRHYN

MANIHIKI

MARQUESAS
ISLANDS

TUAMOTU ARCHIPELAGO

COOK ISLANDS

EASTER ISLAND

0   100   200
STATUTE MILES

RAROTONGA

SOCIETY ISLANDS

BORA BORA

RAIATEA

Papeete
MOOREA

TAHITI

0   50   100
STATUTE MILES

CHAPTER ONE

TAHITI

A Voyager's Dream, Gateway to the Society Islands

TWO HUNDRED YEARS after the first man of the West set foot there, I trod the black volcanic sands of Tahiti's Matavai Bay. A shore verdant with tall coconut palms and feathery casuarina trees received the calm, bright morning. Between beach and coral reef a fisherman paddled his outrigger canoe in the quiet lagoon. The slopes and peaks of the dazzling island leapt luminous in the early light. It was almost too easy to succumb to the scene, like many before me, and forget the rest of the world.

But for a moment my thoughts were two thousand miles west across Moana-nui-o-kiva, "the great ocean of the blue sky." There my friend Olaf Ruhen was traversing the islands and highlands of Melanesia to tell of that of-ten still-remote half of the South Pacific. I was here to tell of the storied Polynesian half, and for this I could choose no better place to begin than Tahiti, an island of legend and song, and largest of all the French-governed Society Islands.

New Zealand-born writers both, with a love for the people and places of the South Pacific, we had problems in telling this vast story. I could envy Ruhen his, for much of Melanesia is still strange to Western man.

Spritsail-rigged fishing canoe cleaves placid water in Tahaa lagoon, 140 miles northwest of Tahiti, largest of French Polynesia's more than 100 scattered islands. One crewman rides the outrigger to balance the craft as the other steers.

PAINTINGS (ABOVE) BY WILLIAM HODGES, MEMBER 1774 COOK EXPEDITION, AND (RIGHT) BY NATHANIEL DANCE, 1776; NATIONAL MARITIME MUSEUM, GREENWICH, ENGLAND

But Polynesia? Like all writers who travel Polynesia now, I carried a weight of words like a ghostly burden: the journals of the voyagers, the rapturous chronicles of the romantics, the novels, the poems, the stories. Polynesia has had so many songs, so many singers; the adjectives have all been used, the superlatives plundered.

Even the Tahitian scene before me, that bright morning, had been immortalized by American Herman Melville: "one mass of shaded tints of green, from beach to mountain top; endlessly diversified with valleys, ridges, glens, and cascades.... the water-falls flash out into the sunlight as if pouring through vertical bowers of verdure.... it seems a fairy world, all fresh and blooming." And it might have been background in a painting by the Frenchman Paul Gauguin.

Outside the South Pacific, mention of Melanesia may produce only a blank stare; but mention of Polynesia can bring a look of longing. The word seems to summon up the jeweled myth of the South Seas: sunny, romantic, utterly without care.

Yet "Polynesia" actually means no more than "many islands." Many islands indeed, islands scattered over more than 15 million square miles of the Pacific in one great triangle with Hawaii at its apex. New Zealand, some 5,000 miles to the southwest of Hawaii, and Easter Island, about the same distance to the southeast, lie at the two other points of the triangle. In prehistoric peopling, these islands testify to man's most remarkable maritime adventure.

H.M.S. Resolution *and* Adventure, *Capt. James Cook's sloops, anchor among canoes in Tahiti's Matavai Bay. Cook (below) led three Pacific expeditions between 1768 and 1779, discovering and charting scores of islands. He died at the hands of Hawaiians in an outburst of violence during a second visit to their islands in 1779.*

Tahitian war fleet of 1774 gathers for a formal inspection — a favorite ceremony of the islanders; a chief in a feathered headdress reviews the armada. Cook saw this flotilla and counted more than 300 canoes.

British explorer and navigator Capt. James Cook, who revealed most of the Pacific to the Western world in the late 18th century, marveled at the achievement. "...it is extraordinary that the same Nation should have spread themselves over all the isles in this Vast Ocean," he said.

Men are still trying to account for those incredible migrations. Challenging questions confront the scientist and the scholar: Where did the Polynesians come from? What route did they follow across the Pacific? How long ago did they arrive among their islands? Once, only legend and tradition offered clues.

Today, archeologists, anthropologists, linguists devote lifetimes to reconstructing the Polynesian story. Most authorities believe that the remote ancestors of the tall, brown-skinned voyagers came from the direction of Southeast Asia and moved slowly east in a series of migrations. But perhaps there will never be final answers. Polynesia means mystery as well as romance. It has also meant high adventure, a voyage into dream.

Almost 2,000 years ago Western man began to speculate on the nature of that part

Tahiti's capital of Papeete, or "basket of waters," rims a wide harbor with newly extended piers where freighters, cruise ships, and vessels of the French Navy can dock. A shopper (left) parks by a billboard-awning on Rue Bonnard.

of the world far to the east of Africa. Geographers and philosophers believed a great continent lay there.

The dream of that elusive southern continent lured Spanish, Dutch, English, and French voyagers. For two and a half centuries after Magellan crossed the Pacific in the 1520's, they ransacked the South Pacific for *Terra Australis Incognita,* the Unknown Southern Land. The Dutch sighting of Australia in 1606 only enhanced the dream. Men pursued it until Captain Cook himself ended the myth in the 1770's with his Pacific explorations; he even ventured far south to polar seas and the fringe of Antarctica.

Though the Unknown Land escaped them, explorers harvested an array of islands—Melanesia to the west, Polynesia to the east.

In 1767 Captain Samuel Wallis arrived off Tahiti in the frigate *Dolphin,* thus fulfilling an island prophecy that strangers would one day arrive in a vessel without an outrigger, and bring change enough for the sacred birds of sea and land to mourn.

For Western man there was change too. The dream of a continent became a dream of islands, a dream of sun-blessed islands inhabited by people fierce in war and gentle in love. "I thought I was transported into the Garden of Eden," said the French explorer Louis Antoine de Bougainville in 1768. "... the truest picture of an arcadia," reported

the English scientist Joseph Banks in 1769.

Tahiti lies at the heart of Polynesia, set like a jewel in the wide and near-empty waters between Australia and South America. Soon the island began to occupy a place in the world's heart too: the island of love, the island of dreams. ". . . in the soul of man there lies one insular Tahiti, full of peace and joy. . ." wrote Melville. "Push not off from that isle, thou canst never return!"

As I walked Tahitian sand by bright lagoon water, in that morning itself as fragile as dream, the old magic seemed undiminished —even if the remembered eloquence of Melville and others like him left me with a faint despair of ever finding my own words. Then my eyes chanced on things new, things changed: flower-screened homes set just back from shore; a radio tower. Planners protect this bay—a headland shut the new Hotel Tahara'a from my gaze—but I could not ignore a jet plane flying low out of the Pacific.

These things had no place in Melville's vision—or in the pristine view of explorers like Bougainville and Cook, the mutineers of William Bligh's *Bounty* who found a paradise here, the missionaries who came to claim the island for Christ, and the French colonists who came to find a more leisurely way of life.

In a very real sense, the jet would guide

Ruhen and me in telling our stories, for we— voyagers of the present—would visit mainly those islands lying on international air routes.

I said a lingering goodbye to Matavai Bay and drove five miles and two centuries toward modern Papeete, capital of French Polynesia, into a frantic boom and bustle strange to the tropical Pacific. Until the 1950's Papeete was much as it had been for a century: sleepy port and island trading center; a village of peace and charm on an island remote from the world. Then in 1959 the French began construction of an airport and told the garden of Eden it must start paying for itself. "When you have a remote paradise, you have no tourists," a spokesman said.

The move was not entirely welcome either among indigenous Tahitians or old-time Europeans; their surrender to the world was often unwilling.

"We had an easy life where money meant little, time even less," a long-resident Frenchman explained to me. But they had to surrender, it seemed, if the island was not to remain a poor relative of metropolitan France. The new airport smothered Faaa lagoon with a wide ribbon of coral, jets flew in, hotels multiplied, tourists arrived by the thousand.

Now the roar of traffic drowns the reef's old serenade. I make a point of never driving through downtown Papeete—life is thrilling enough as a pedestrian. Thousands of cars and motor scooters jam the roads. The island of dreams has taken to wheels with an enthusiasm sometimes frightening. At best Tahitian driving is adequate; at worst it has a kind of kamikaze panache. Cabdrivers seem to think nothing of passing on narrow roads against streams of oncoming traffic—to the sound of squealing brakes and blaring horns.

Tourism is one reason for the affluence reflected by wheeled traffic. Another is the

Acacia trees shade Papeete's Rue Dumont d'Urville, shared by cars and motor scooters during the afternoon rush. In traffic jams rivaling those of many bustling Western cities, 27,000 bicycles and motorbikes, 8,000 motorcycles, and 25,000 autos clog Tahiti's 130 miles of roads. At left, a passenger casually balanced on a bicycle carries home fish fresh from the market.

decision of France to conduct nuclear tests on remote atolls in its portion of Polynesia, and to station an estimated 5,000 military and civilian personnel in the territory. This meant big payrolls and construction jobs. Today the island of love lies shadowed, more than most places, by the mushroom cloud. The world has arrived with a vengeance.

"But it's no use mourning the past," American resident David Cave told me. "Not that I don't, sometimes. After all, I remember this place as a quiet village. As recently as the early 1950's horse-drawn freight wagons and buggies were a common sight on Papeete's streets." He left off to vanish into some personal dream for a moment, then said, "Today you can't even get parking space."

Tahitian Frenchman Guy Deflesselle put it another way. "My family came here in the 19th century for peace and quiet and an easy life," he lamented. "Now I think life might be easier, less of a race, home in France."

A stocky, smiling Tahitian taxi driver named Émile put it a third way. "I didn't want the change," he said. "But now it's come. . . ." He shrugged expressively and put his hand out for my fare.

TAHITIAN PRICES can be as breathtaking as the island's scenery, and the two are linked. "After all," more than one businessman explained to me, "if this is the world's most beautiful island, people are prepared to pay handsomely to see it." And pay they do. In 1966 some 16,000 tourists stayed here, a thousand percent increase over 1959. About 49,000 came by air alone in 1970.

What is the powerful myth that brings visitors flooding here, despite all change? It is, after all, largely the creation of writers and artists: men who believed Tahiti offered the world a new and gentle way to live, and celebrated the island accordingly. Their passionate prose and verse, their paintings, made Tahiti indelible in the world's mind: a synonym for romance, for sunlit freedom, for Polynesia itself.

But the new, breathless Papeete can be loved and enjoyed for itself as it is, as well as for what it has been. Imagine a pie with a piquant crust of French pastry; inside is the Polynesian flavor of marinated raw fish and coconut milk, blended with Chinese chow mein, and deeper still the wild pagan taste of *fei,* the red mountain banana that thrives in the island's steeply pinnacled and virtually uninhabited interior. The town's population of 30,000 — European, Chinese, and indigenous Tahitian — give it distinction and color. So do its restaurants, waterfront bars, and night spots.

I took in the boisterous 19th-century atmosphere of Quinn's Tahitian Hut, where seamen and Tahitian girls dance the wild, hip-jolting *tamure* with all its original fervor to the drumbeat and electric twang of a band set high behind the circular bar.

The Polynesians' famed love of dancing also finds expression at the nearby Bar Pitate and the dim-lit Bar Zizou. These places sometimes take on the appearance of Western night spots when flower-garlanded islanders and visiting travelers swing vigorously into the latest successor to the twist.

The golden-brown Tahitian girl, or *vahine,* has had her charms sung, by voyager and visitor, for two centuries — everyman's dream of romance. With thousands of visitors now jetting to the island, I couldn't help wondering if the vahine might have become a little tired of her enviable reputation. Wasn't it just a little too much to live up to?

"Yes and no," one girl laughed. "If you worried about these things that were said, it might be. But then we don't worry. Listen to all those flowery things they say about Tahitian girls and you just become bored with the whole thing."

But it's doubtful if the outside world will become bored with the girls of Tahiti — their flowing walk, hips and shoulders swaying, supple figures seldom clad in more

Fiery hibiscus tucked in her hair, Vaitiara, a Tahitian-Chinese, dances the hip-jolting ta-mure to the pulsing beat of drums and the sharp clapping of hands. With skirt and pompons made of shredded bark of the purau *tree, she performs in Tahiti with members of the Tamaeva group. After observing the wildly uninhibited dance, Captain Cook wrote that the people would "shake themselves in a very whimsical manner."*

than brightly flower-patterned cotton shifts. The island still has them by the hundred, the laughing children of nature, exactly as promised on the travel posters.

In another respect Papeete remains unchanged: It is still a haven for the adventurous. Yachts of several nations, paused in long Pacific hauls, moor along the Quai Bir-Hackeim—right in the heart of town, where a bust of Bougainville symbolizes the spirit of the navigator. And across the road, in the sidewalk cafe Vaima, I found adventurers swapping yarns of storms and islands. Here too some of the "characters" congregate, though the beachcomber is a fast-dying breed, unwanted by the authorities. Still, by subterfuge or chance, some who come to visit manage to stay on.

Racing bicyclists speed through Papeete's streets during the annual celebration of the fall of the Bastille on July 14, 1789. The two-week fete attracts participants from all over French Polynesia to a Coney Island atmosphere of singing and dancing, feasting and festivity. Poised to hurl a steel-tipped javelin, a contestant from Tahaa takes aim at a coconut atop a 30-foot pole. A row of bazaars attracts sidewalk crowds.

"Could I take Madison Avenue again?" said one young American. "You're kidding. My life only began when my boat sailed without me."

By contrast there was the sad-faced Englishman whose damaged boat had been tied up two months for repairs. "It's not at all what I expected," he said moodily. "The girls don't

come out to greet you with bunches of fruit any more."

As I sat beside them sipping cool beer—Tahiti's most popular drink—I looked out on the quay and hoped jet age and building boom never push the yachts away from central Papeete. Like Quinn's Hut, they make a genuine link with Tahiti's past.

I felt that past again as I traveled around the island, among the "clear, warm colours" that so moved and inspired Gauguin. Even under the sullen sky of the rainy season, Tahiti glows as if with some inner warmth left over from the old and now extinguished volcanic fires that pushed the island's greatest peaks well over a mile above the sea. But it is the flowers that really warm the atmosphere: waxy frangipani, exuberant bou-

gainvillea, the fragrant gardenia called *tiare Tahiti,* and uncounted varieties of hibiscus.

The hourglass-shaped 407 square miles of the island—called in myth a great fish possessed by the soul of a lovely maiden—are sliced by scores of bright rivers; waterfalls gleam as they unfold down the slopes. A circular coast road now encloses most of the island, extending prongs on either side of the Taiarapu Peninsula.

This is the island that charms today's jet traveler as much as it did yesterday's ocean-weary. I walked through the small park—shady with casuarinas, pandanus trees, and palms—that now graces Point Venus, the northeast tip of Matavai Bay. Cook left the place its name by building a fort here while befriending Tahitians and observing the

21

transit of the planet Venus on June 3, 1769.

Cook wrestled with unfamiliar Tahitian customs; Protestant missionaries, who followed the explorer to the island in the London Missionary Society ship *Duff* in 1797, wrestled with Tahitian souls—with eventual spectacular success. The Tahitians are still nearly 55 percent Protestant, though Catholicism made gains when the island came under French rule in 1842. In that year a French officer, Rear Admiral Abel Du Petit-Thouars, arrived in Tahiti and induced influential chiefs to sign a document making their island a protectorate of France.

As elsewhere in Polynesia, the arrival of Europeans brought devastating diseases. The population shrank. Gradually, pagan temples tumbled, and old ways vanished. But the mountainous beauty of the coral-ringed island remained.

The northeast coast is rugged, rocky, surf-beaten. Villages are caught in a coastal strip between surf and sharp slopes, some patterned with small vanilla plantations. The south side is gentle, with calm lagoons, spacious gardens, coconut plantations, and grazing cattle. This sharp contrast seems to echo the simultaneously fierce and gentle nature of the Polynesian himself; for me, no other island better symbolizes his character.

Some of the warmth that distinguished that character may have gone now. "Once we used to smile at every stranger, and offer hospitality," a middle-aged Tahitian explained to me. "But now there are too many strangers. We haven't grown unfriendly. We're just overwhelmed." He paused. "But I think we still love life just as much. I'd sooner have a family feast than a television set."

T HE TAHITIAN'S FAMED LOVE of life sprang from a sharp sense of life's brevity. Says a well-known Tahitian proverb: "The palm tree shall grow, the coral spread, but man shall cease to be."

That life-love was bound to fascinate artist and writer. My journey could easily have become a pilgrimage to the memory of writers who made this island a glowing legend: Melville, Robert Louis Stevenson, Pierre Loti, Rupert Brooke, Somerset Maugham,

Mount Tohivea, 3,960 feet high, towers above sailboats bunched for the start of a regatta. White-winged 420's and blue-sailed Rascals dominate this Sunday race in Papeete harbor. A French sailor (above) returns to his ship after shore leave, garlanded with a lei made of shells.

Charles Nordhoff and James Norman Hall —the Americans who wrote *Mutiny on the Bounty* and many other tales of the South Sea.

Maugham gave literature *The Moon and Sixpence,* his fictional version of Gauguin's life. And the island forever haunted him; shortly before his death in England in 1965 he said, "If I was granted one last wish it would be to swim again in the crystalline, cool waters of some South Seas lagoon." In tribute to Maugham's memory, I swam the Mataiea lagoon and recalled joyous lines the young English poet Rupert Brooke had written there in a letter to a friend: "Tonight we will put scarlet flowers in our hair and sing strange, slumbrous South Sea songs . . . bathe in a soft lagoon by moonlight, and eat great squelchy tropical fruits. . . ."

I found Brooke almost forgotten today, unlike Maugham—and unlike Gauguin, who chose to live like a native and was rejected by fellow Frenchmen on the island. A street

in Papeete bears his name, and a school; and above all, to the east of the island, at Papeari, a splendid new museum tells the story of his life and displays the work of painters living in Polynesia today.

In the museum grounds I paused before a large stone tiki, a sacred image in human form. Tahitians had told me of the powerful and deadly *tapu,* or sacred spell, which rests upon her squat features. "Some tiki are dead," they said. "Others still live. This one lives; the stone still breathes." So strong was this belief that no Tahitian would help move the tiki from Papeete, where once it sat. Four Marquesan islanders did the job in 1965.

Most of Tahiti's pagan mysteries have fled. Just one *marae,* or temple platform of ancient belief, the one called Arahurahu, 15 miles south of Papeete, is anywhere near its original form. Its open-air altars, where human sacrifice was offered to Polynesian gods, are

built of hundreds of small black volcanic stones. The temple stands in the quiet of a ferny valley under high peaks.

It was time to see the powerful center of ancient belief; time to see more of the other Society Islands. My plane roared off the strip and climbed above multicolored reef and lagoon. Behind me, the peaks of Tahiti shrank quickly into the sea. A 100-mile flight northwest across the waters Polynesians called "Sea of the Moon" offered me sight of the blunt, patchily green heights of Raiatea, second-largest island in the Societies after Tahiti.

Traditionally first-settled of the Society group, and once its spiritual and political center, Raiatea was known as "mother of lands." At the village of Uturoa, a lively, laughing marketplace and quiet Chinese-owned shops still call in voyagers, in motor-propelled outriggers now, from neighboring islands. Here

I sampled with pleasure some of the old sleepy island calm the jet age has banished from Tahiti itself.

But Raiatea called further into the past, when I journeyed swiftly down the long lagoon by motorboat and arrived at the cape where once stood the great Polynesian temple of Taputapu-atea. In pre-European times, the priestly ritual and theology of this place

Coronation of a king—an ancient ritual re-enacted in the wavering light of torches—evokes Tahiti's past on a reconstructed open-air temple platform, the Marae Arahurahu. *The new king, in a headdress of feathers and shells, sits between wooden pillars surmounted by tikis, sacred images in human form (detail, lower right). The high priest, in similar headdress, occupies a position behind him. Slat structures commemorate human sacrifices. The basalt tiki (right), which some Tahitians believe still lives, stands nine feet tall and weighs more than two tons. Carved centuries ago on Raivavae Island, it has stood since 1965 on the grounds of the Musée Gauguin at Papeari, on the east coast of Tahiti. High humidity in this new location near the sea caused mottling of the soft stone.*

influenced the entire Society group and islands beyond. All that remain now are eroding and tumbled stones where lizards and land crabs skitter beneath a green canopy of palms.

"No villager would touch anything here, even a small stone, so great is the respect for the tapu of the place," a Tahitian friend told me.

Yet it wasn't difficult for my imagination to summon up scenes once enacted there: human sacrifices, investiture of kings, invocations to the gods. And, above all, the blessings accorded departing voyagers. For Raiatea, according to tradition, dispatched migrant canoes to Hawaii in the north and New Zealand in the southwest, distances over 2,000 miles. Religious intolerance may have driven some upon their marvelous voyages of colonization, much as the Pilgrims were driven across the Atlantic.

Now the gods are gone, the drumbeats have ceased, the voyaging is done. The island is quiet, a place of ghosts and legends, with a feeling of age and sadness.

"Yet I prefer it here," elderly Tahitian Sonny Chave told me. "Tahiti has too many noisy *popaa* [Europeans] these days, too many cars. And here I can take strength from the history of my people."

Together we watched the summit of 3,389-foot Mount Temehani emerge briefly from rain cloud into the flame-red light of sunset. From that extinct volcano, I recalled, the fierce god Oro — ultimately the most powerful in the Society Islands — had been born. "And upon that peak too grows the sacred white flower *tiare apetahi,*" Sonny said. "It grows nowhere else in the world, and can't be transplanted. It has the five fingers of a beautiful Tahitian girl who fell in love with the son of a royal chief and died of a broken heart because she could not hope to marry him. The flower is born at dawn and perishes at nightfall."

No one who feels for Polynesia and its tradition can fail to be moved by Raiatea. I watched its wild, broken shore slip away beneath a shining wing with a feeling of loss, and the sensation that I had come near the heart of the Polynesian mysteries.

But within minutes the great three-peaked bulk of islet-garlanded Bora Bora called attention across the sea, much as it must have called those first voyagers. To me, no Polynesian island looms more dramatically from the sea. And air travel, for once, cannot steal the majesty of this approach, for the airstrip rests on a *motu,* or reef islet, and the traveler must

Leaky Tiki *belies its name, ferrying guests of Moorea's Bali Hai Hotel across the island's breeze-rippled lagoon. Surf marks the offshore reef. Airline stewardesses, staying overnight at the hotel, enjoy fringe benefits of Pacific flights.*
MICHAEL E. LONG, NATIONAL GEOGRAPHIC STAFF

board a launch to reach the main shore.

Porpoises leaped around us as we crossed the lagoon. "To show we are welcome," a delighted Tahitian beside me observed. With little flat and cultivable land beneath immense volcanic bluffs, life has always meant struggle on Bora Bora. According to island tradition, Tahitians once sent troublemakers into lifetime exile there; in time the outcasts became the most feared warriors in east Polynesia, raiding neighboring islands by night in canoes with muffled paddles.

Now the island's freshest memories are of a war that never actually touched its reef: During World War II, thousands of Americans moved in to make a rear base for the Pacific fighting. Today the ruins of that occupation crumble along the shore, fast blending with the ruins of the island's pagan temples. And tourism, still moving lightly, has begun a longer, more significant occupation; islanders are relearning their half-forgotten wartime English.

Early one morning I paddled an outrigger across a serene lagoon and then put on mask and flippers. I dived through dissolving rainbows of tropic fish into the wonderland of the Polynesian lagoon. Grotto and castle of bright, many-hued living coral, lit with tangling skeins of sunlight, trembled around me. At my least movement clouds of fish exploded, heaping color on color. The shades of the world above seemed pastel and tame when I surfaced.

I eased the outrigger on to the tiny reef islet of Motu Tapu, a 250-yard length of coral debris held together by coconut palms, which has enriched man's fantasy life. Here in 1930 Robert Flaherty and German director Friedrich Murnau made the motion picture *Tabu,* one of a long line of films with lush and lovely Polynesian background that gave visual form to the literary romances of the South Seas. Yet there might never have been camera, or actor, upon that coral shore. I might, in the cool of a golden morning, have been the first man. To each man his own Polynesia. Mine shall always be a beached outrigger beneath the palms, an empty island.

This was the magic that the first Polynesian voyagers knew. These islands were nature's fair reward to the fearless, to men prepared to sail hundreds of miles with prayer, hope, and knowledge of the turbulent sea's language. The people of Bora Bora, more than most Polynesians it seems to me, retain the old instinct for navigation. I talked with Clark Reynolds, an American then a resident, who often sailed with them.

"On trips among the nearby islands," he said, "I've sometimes awakened them in the middle of the night and they've told me, without even thinking the question over, just where we are, and guided the boat in dark and storm through an invisible gap in an invisible reef—into the lagoon and safety."

Back on Tahiti, I watched the superb sunset beyond the peaks of Moorea and tossed a coin. Some travelers have argued that it

Tahitian women bear mangoes and flowers in Paul Gauguin's "Les Seins aux Fleurs Rouges," painted in 1899. The 43-year-old Parisian stockbroker abandoned career and family in 1891 to seek paradise and to paint on Tahiti. There, he wrote, "the landscape with its violent, pure colors dazzled and blinded me." The women of Tahiti continue to captivate travelers with their gentle beauty and supple grace.

28

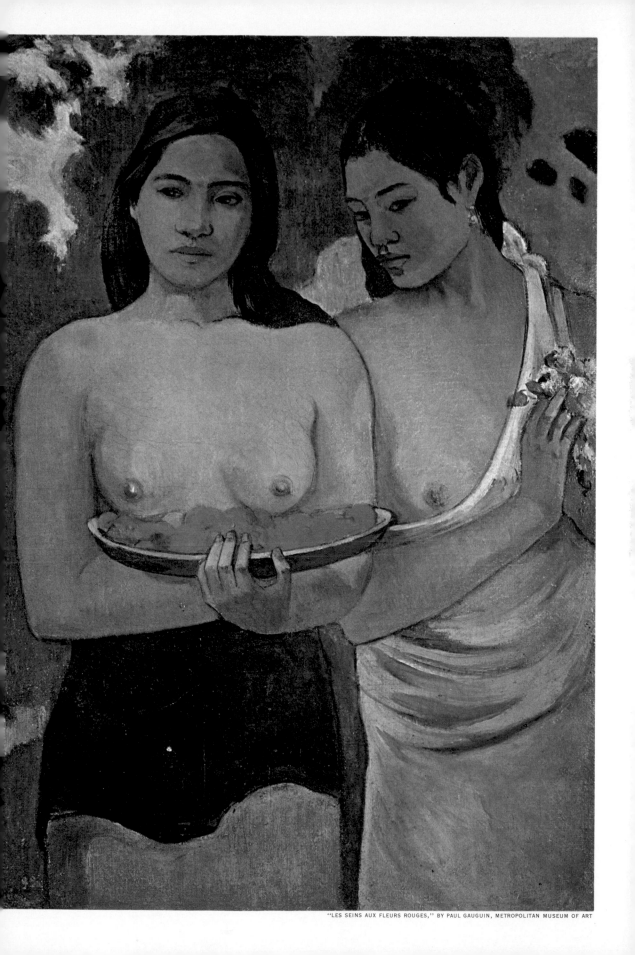

"LES SEINS AUX FLEURS ROUGES," BY PAUL GAUGUIN, METROPOLITAN MUSEUM OF ART

is best not to cross that narrow strait between Tahiti and Moorea, that one should rest content forever with the perfection of the distant image. Could the reality of the island ever measure up?

The coin came down heads. Next morning, I was on a launch with guitar-strumming Tahitians — and the reality did not disappoint me. There is a lunatic grandeur about mountainous Moorea, as if fiery nature, in the birth of the world, had taken it into her head to try everything, to twist and bludgeon mountains into every conceivable shape.

On this friendly island the old Tahitian greeting of *Ia ora na* — "life to you" — still has real meaning, sung out to me along the roadside by families gathering and splitting coconuts for copra. The sweet, clinging smell of copra distinguishes most Polynesian islands as much as friendliness. The value of the oil from the dried white meat of the coconut was recognized in the 19th century, when copra became a major South Pacific industry.

When processed for its oil, in factories thousands of miles distant, copra becomes part of soap, cosmetics, margarine, and many other products. It has never meant great wealth: A villager needs about 4,500 nuts for

Schooner Eryx II, *out of Southampton, England, and bound around the world, anchors in Moorea's Papetoai Bay. The waters of French Polynesia, rarely troubled by hurricanes and offering unsurpassed sailing weather six months of the year, beckon to yachtsmen from all over the world.*

a ton of copra, worth about $140. But it has meant modest income for Pacific islanders with no other cash crop. On Moorea, though, the thick smell of drying copra is often subdued by the scent of vanilla beans: A hundred tons or more are exported annually from the Society Islands, principally Raiatea, Tahaa,

Huahine, and Moorea. Both industries, however, have begun to look tiny beside the booming growth of tourism.

Yet Moorea still seems more nine hundred miles than nine from docks and jet planes and traffic-noisy streets. After the island's quiet, Papeete was too much for me when I returned. So I took a car down to the south of Tahiti, and then took to my feet. I had glimpsed the island's spectacular basalt interior from the air—greenly packed about the great peaks of Orohena, Aorai, and Diadème —but now I wanted to see it more closely.

I followed a muddy track through a cattle-grazed coconut plantation and ascended a steep, narrow valley where a swift river tossed up white water. Bursting through vegetation I found, surprisingly, a family who had made a home here, far from the easy life of the shore. Their house was walled with bamboo and thatched with coconut fronds. Large-leafed breadfruit trees shed dull yellow globes of fruit; bulging bunches of bananas ripened on the stem; taro flourished in swampy ground beside the river.

"We came up here," the sturdy man of the house explained, "because there is too much change down there on the coast, too many people. One day we might go back, when the French leave and Tahiti belongs once more to Tahitians. In the meantime we work this old family land we have claimed again."

I found in the valley not only a vestige of red-blooded Tahitian nationalism, but also the old Polynesian hospitality. Food and drink appeared before me as I sat cross-legged on a mat of coconut fronds: pork, wrapped in banana leaves and roasted in an *ahimaa,* or underground oven; baked taro root, the starch food favored throughout Polynesia; and *umara,* or sweet potato. To finish there was *poe,* a pudding found in one form or another in most of Polynesia, a baked concoction of arrowroot flour flavored with banana or pawpaw and sauced with the salted milk of coconuts.

A popaa, they insisted as we ate, was rare in this valley; and never before had they seen one wandering the rugged interior without a guide. If ever I cared to come again and stay...

I began regretting my appointment with that suddenly incongruous jet. Cheerful children buzzed about us in a noisy swarm. "All yours?" I asked.

"Most," the man of the house said. "But two belong to my brother. He gave them away to us when his wife died." He pulled a shy, half-naked tot to his side. "And there's this one from my sister—a little one who just decided herself to come and live with us for a while, maybe for good."

Seemingly casual Polynesian behavior toward marriage and children has always perplexed Westerners. Yet it was plain these youngsters, whoever their parents, would never lack love. For in Polynesia love of children does not mean exclusive love of one's own; it means love of all children. And children, often enough, herald a marriage rather than follow it. A childless couple will be given babies by sympathetic relatives.

It was time to say goodbye to the friendly family and push farther up the valley, amid wild coffee bushes and fragrant lime trees. I seemed to be finding the old Polynesia in places I least expected it, in this valley, even at my hotel in Papeete, which styled itself *L'Hôtel le Plus Sélect de la Polynésie.* There, in the evening, a few yards from tourists sipping expensive cocktails, Tahitian boys and girls gathered discreetly in the darkness of the hotel wharf to sing softly and fish the lagoon.

As I climbed, the island grew wilder around me; banana patches thinned and disappeared. Instead there was prolific fern, and a dense net of foliage above. I forded the river again and again as I traveled deeper into the valley.

Finally, I could go no farther. The silence of Tahiti's interior was as thick as the forest. The sun gleamed on the river; I dropped to my knees to cool my face and drink from the waters of Polynesia which still run pure.

Craggy mountains of Bora Bora—Pahia (left) and Temanu—climb from the dark ocean floor, break the surface, and finally peak at more than 2,000 feet above sea level. Teava-nui harbor separates the island from neighboring Tupua, a narrow reef islet. Bora Bora's slopes and valleys blossom with fragrant hibiscus (left), found in uncounted varieties on nearly all Pacific islands.

CHAPTER TWO

THE
COOK ISLANDS

The Lonely Places

FIVE DAYS from sight of an island, with only sea birds for company upon a silent ocean, the tiny copra boat rolled north toward the Equator. Six hundred miles behind us lay Rarotonga, largest and most prosperous of the Cook Islands; somewhere ahead was one of the remote atolls of the northern Cooks. As the sun dipped in the west, hymns rose from deck passengers at evening worship.

I stood on the bridge beside thickset Fijian Archie Pickering, skipper of the 200-ton *Akatere*. "We're not far from Manihiki," he said. "Time to take things more slowly. We don't want to miss it in the dark."

He scanned the still-empty ocean in the fading light. "Not such a bright prospect if you're running low on food and water.

There's not an island in the northern Cooks that isn't easy to miss. They're so low you've got to be within 12 miles to see one — at least the tops of their coconut palms. It's only 25 miles between Manihiki and Rakahanga, for example. Traveling between, you can lose sight of both. An open sailing cutter making the trip finished up 2,100 miles west, in the New Hebrides, two months later — with only three of seven men surviving."

Comprehend the Cook Islands, 93 square

Pearl-shell divers of Manihiki, a remote atoll in the northern Cook Islands, soar toward the surface of their luminous lagoon. Mother-of-pearl and copra bring income here. Fruits and vegetables thrive in the more fertile southern Cooks.

miles of land and sand sprinkled across 750,000 square miles of ocean, and you go a long way toward comprehending the immensity of the Polynesian achievement. Fifteen specks dot the map between Tahiti and Samoa—the largest a mere 26 square miles and the smallest a minuscule 100 acres. Polynesians knew virtually all of them long before Europe's voyagers had ventured out of sight of Atlantic shores.

On that copra boat, making a top speed of around seven knots, about the pace of a Tahitian outrigger under sail in fair weather, I

Stricken brigantine Yankee *lies abandoned off Avarua, capital of Rarotonga and administrative center of the Cooks.* Yankee, *often featured in the* NATIONAL GEOGRAPHIC, *ran aground when her anchor lines snapped in a gale in 1964 (right). Treacherous Pacific shoals and reefs have claimed many unlucky vessels through the centuries.*

was at last able to settle a prickly controversy—at least to my own satisfaction. Some scholars have argued convincingly that Polynesian settlement of the Pacific must have been accidental, the result of a long series of

drift voyages. The Polynesians, they say, setting courses by sun and stars and wind and wave, could not have had the precise measure of longitude needed to conduct deliberate voyages over great distances.

No one denies that the Polynesians could —and did—navigate their large sail-rigged double canoes on trips between islands some 200 miles apart. Authorities who subscribe to the theory of accidental voyages believe those islands that lay at greater distances were colonized by travelers swept off course on short trips, or by exiles searching blindly for a new island to settle.

It all seems eminently reasonable until one actually gets out on the huge Pacific, away from libraries, and considers the fantastic fact that there was scarcely a habitable island in this emptiness that they did not claim.

To me, this fact alone strongly supports those scholars who believe settlement of the South Pacific could only have come from a tradition and ritual of deliberate voyaging, from systematic sea search generation after generation. Each new voyager would inherit only the memory of successful voyages. The South Pacific, after all, would hide failures well—much as the swift dark now hid Manihiki Atoll as we approached.

Aboard that antique copra boat I felt a world away from scholarly debate, the jet-age Pacific, and the tourist traffic of Tahiti, now some 900 miles to the southeast.

The feeling intensified next morning when I scrambled from my bunk. The ship was drifting, engines idling. From the rail I looked

FRANK J. DUNN (BELOW) AND ROBERT B. JOHNSON

People of the Cooks: Boys on tiny Mauke Island ride a horse to school (1), and a lean-faced mother-of-pearl diver on Manihiki Atoll squints against the sun (2). Most atoll dwellers are very young or aging. Many have left their remote homes to seek opportunity on more prosperous islands or in New Zealand. On Rakahanga, a girl (3) pedals a bicycle, a principal means of transportation in the Cooks. A Rarotonga boy (4) pauses at play on his lush green isle, and an impish Manihiki girl nestles in a window (5). A Rarotongan (6) wears the cap of the Life Boys, an organization like the Boy Scouts. A silver cross gleams at the throat of a young girl (7), and an older churchgoer (8), Bible at her side, rests in the sun on Penrhyn Atoll. Most of the islanders worship as Protestants. A fisherman (9) scans Manihiki lagoon, famed for its fine mother-of-pearl. A Rarotongan (10) performs a canoe dance. A nimble-fingered weaver makes a hat (11). Mosquito netting blurs the features of a baby-sitter (12), and a youngster home from school fondles her sister (13). When emigrating, many parents let young offspring stay with older relatives. On Manihiki a grinning boy (14) holds a pig, a delicacy throughout the islands, and a youngster bites her lip during a game of paddle ball (15). In Sunday best, a Penrhyn man (16) relaxes with a smoke.

WILLIAM ALBERT ALLARD

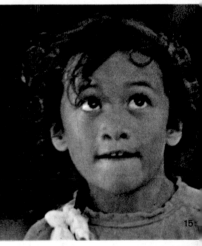

Eyes on the ball, cricket players of Rarotonga battle on a field fenced by sunlit palms. Missionaries and New Zealanders introduced the game to the islands, along with tennis, basketball, rugby, and boxing. The Cook Islands Sports Association supervises organized sports. Furious chop (above) attests the islanders' enthusiasm.

out upon a pale isle vivid in the dawn, palms shot through with rays of rising sun, dark figures moving along the glistening beach.

I seemed to have slipped back two centuries, into an ocean of uncharted islands, the Pacific as once it was — and often can still be, in the lonely places. And no places in the South Pacific are lonelier than the atolls. When the Polynesian voyager searched this ocean for scraps of land, he found two basic types of island — "high" and "low." The high islands are volcanic, sometimes little more than sea-bitten lumps of rock, sometimes, like Tahiti, dramatically spired with mountains fringed by fertile lowland. The low islands are coral; a few of them rise as much as 300 feet out of the water, but most are atolls no higher than 20 feet.

Limited arable land on even the fruitful

high islands made it necessary for the Polynesian to settle all the low islands he could find, no matter how barren and uninviting. Seven of the low islands of the Cooks are atolls, most in the classic doughnut shape — a low necklace of islets strung along a coral reef enclosing a lagoon.

Charles Darwin's theory, accepted by most earth scientists today, holds that atolls are but the remnants of once high volcanic islands like Tahiti that, through millenniums, sank into the ocean as the sea floor subsided beneath them. Coral polyps kept pace with the subsidence, building their limestone structures slowly upward on the island's encircling barrier reef. Finally the last vestiges of the island itself disappeared, bequeathing that marvel of nature called the atoll.

Now it was time to shoot the reef, for Manihiki's lagoon has no entrance. I left *Akatere* for a slender, trembling longboat. Our steersman eyed the surf that seethed across the dangerous coral, waiting his moment. *"Oe!"* he cried. "Pull!" Oars swung with precision, lifting us atop a wave high enough to carry us all the way to shore. Surf exploded around us. Then, suddenly, we were safe, and surrounded by islanders helping us ashore, their first visitors in two months.

Atoll-dwellers have learned survival the hard way on their infertile accretions of coral. Their basic diet, all year, has always consisted of coconuts and fish, breadfruit and taro — these days supplemented by canned meat and flour. Without the fruits of volcanic islands, atoll people also lack the abundance of flowers. The first law of survival is adaptation, and that adaptation was vividly symbolized by the *'ei* — equivalent of the Hawaiian lei — which a Manihiki girl dropped about my neck; a string of tiny seashells formed a perfect illusion of flowers.

Today the economic survival of an atoll such as Manihiki depends on slender resources. Here some 650 people, with two square miles of land and a lagoon five miles across, earn income from copra and mother-of-pearl shell. From the landing, I walked a quarter of a mile through Tauhunu village to the serene lagoon, where I joined a party of shell divers. Manihiki's divers are among

Born to the sea, a Manihiki diver sur-
faces with coral-encrusted shells. An
unbroken reef fences the lagoon, keeping
sharks out. Men dive year-round for
mother-of-pearl shell, exported for cutting into jewelry and buttons. A Rarotongan (below) stalks fish in shallows.

Patched cloth sail drives tuna fishermen of Penrhyn Atoll across

silver sea. This outrigger's design remains little changed from that of craft described by Captain Cook.

43

Polynesia's best—most achieve depths of 80 to 120 feet with ease. Out on the lagoon, within the atoll's ring of 39 coral islets, I used mask and snorkel to watch them glide with unbelievable leisure over the lagoon floor, more than a dozen fathoms below. They plucked the shell as they might dark blooms from a bright rainbow forest in fairyland.

I returned to *Akatere* and the thickening smell of 30 tons of Manihiki copra. Tears of farewell stained brown cheeks as the ship pushed out. A couple of dozen young people were taking leave of their native atoll, perhaps forever, to remake their lives in Rarotonga or New Zealand.

After a brief copra stop at Rakahanga, we set out for Penrhyn, northernmost of the Cooks, and one of the South Pacific's loneliest isles. No ship had called in four months. The people of the atoll, some 700, were out of canned meat, sugar, rice, flour, soap, and tobacco. When we stood off the lagoon entrance after nightfall, the lights of sailboats bobbed toward us. Islanders leaped aboard with the cry of *"Avaava!"*—"Cigarettes!"

Next morning we sailed into the 108-square-mile lagoon. The passes here give entrance to sharks as well as ships, so diving is a perilous occupation. Once diving here was big business—for pearls and shell—but now Japan's cultured pearls have driven the natural Penrhyn pearl off the market. There is little incentive today to risk shark attack, though some men still do for the mother-of-pearl they can collect. I journeyed upon the lagoon in a sailboat with three divers who promised a day to remember.

We prayed before we dived. Once it might have been a chant to Tangaroa, god of the sea; today it is a prayer to the Christian God. "Something to keep in mind," one explained, "is that if the shark attacks you, be careful to kick it in the nose, not the teeth—you can lose a leg that way."

My enthusiasm waned, more so when they speared some small fish, deliberately leaving blood on the water. "After all," they said cheerfully, "you'd be disappointed not to see a shark or two."

A shark or two? Within minutes there were twenty, more each moment. For once I could not appreciate the beauties of the coral lagoon with its dazzling fish life. I scrambled out of the water, fast, and back into the boat.

Though shark attacks have been many, fatalities are few. Barren Penrhyn Atoll breeds a hardy human being. The island has survived plundering by last century's Peruvian slavers, and, because of the loss of the pearl market, a precipitous drop in prosperity over the past twenty years; the sharks seem insignificant.

They seemed insignificant, too, when I joined villagers in their Sunday *uapo*, or hymnfest, with rival teams of islanders trying to outsing each other in the evening cool, seated in the courtyard of the Protestant pastor's home. Most Polynesians, more than a century after conversion by missionaries,

With slender sticks and a rugby ball, children on Mauke Island improvise a game on the lawn of their gleaming church. The London Missionary Society began establishing schools and places of worship for Cook Islanders in 1823. Today, the church remains a dominant force in their lives. On Penrhyn Atoll a family awaits the beginning of the service, and a smiling girl arrives with her Bible.

WILLIAM ALBERT ALLARD

retain the early Christian fervor; and none more than Penrhyn's isolated people. The rich, wild resonance of their voices — and their faith — rose amid tears and laughter into a Pacific night thick with stars.

There were hymns again next day, when the islanders sadly watched *Akatere*'s departure. Perhaps they would see another boat in four months, if their copra made a stop worthwhile; but in the past decade they have gone as long as eight months without a call.

Now we faced the 737-mile journey from the austere and lonely life of the atolls to the flower-fragrant island of Rarotonga. A storm roared out of the South Pacific; huge waves crashed over *Akatere*. Speed dwindled to two knots and less. Such slight little trading ships

Islanders on Atiu (left) and Rakahanga load sacks of oranges and bags of copra — principal export crops of the Cooks. Cargo ships will take most of the yield to New Zealand; part of the fruit will go to Rarotonga's juice cannery.

as *Akatere*, without radar, often survive on a skipper's instinct in these hurricane-haunted waters. Well off regular shipping lanes, we were hundreds of miles from possible help.

The storm passed, and on the eighth day the green heights and spiky peaks of Rarotonga rose fitfully sunlit beyond the mist and waves. Rarotonga is a smaller, neater version of Tahiti; quieter, too, and perhaps lovelier in its symmetry. A 20-mile coast road took me around the island by motor scooter

WILLIAM ALBERT ALLARD

in less than an hour, through villages often still shy with strangers. More than 5,000 acres of cultivated coastal country surrender suddenly to a dense and razory cluster of peaks, a dozen more than 1,000 feet high.

I climbed one of them in the cool of morning. With its distinctively needling summit, 1,590-foot Mount Ikurangi means "tail of the sky"; it was so sacred to early Rarotongans, and so beloved as a symbol of their balmy island, that when they voyaged south to the new and harsher land of New Zealand they bestowed its name on a score of heights.

From my narrow foothold on the summit I looked down on Rarotonga, on the circling reef that still holds the wrecked brigantine *Yankee.* Plantations of orange, tangerine,

lemon, and grapefruit trees — mainstay of the island's economy — darkly greened the slopes below. Here and there were large tomato patches. Houses stood among the palms. Commanding attention too was the village of Avarua, seat of administration for the tiny self-governing state of the Cook Islands.

Avarua is just beginning to lose the atmosphere of a 19th-century South Sea island trading post — an atmosphere given by wooden buildings, corrugated-iron rooftops, half-shanty cargo sheds, and a rambling one-level hotel. Change is still modest: a new post office and government building, a department store and coffee bar on the seafront, only a few yards from beached outrigger canoes among old ironwood trees. And just yards from the village's first hotel a cannery juices Cook Island oranges and pineapples for the New Zealand market.

Though Spanish explorers saw the northern atolls as early as 1595 when Alvaro de Mendaña de Neyra discovered tiny Pukapuka, the more populous southern Cooks awaited later voyagers. Cook charted five islands in the 1770's, enough for the entire group to receive his name; but he missed Rarotonga. Island tradition says *Bounty* mutineers were the first Europeans to see Rarotonga, anchoring off the coast in 1789 to barter with the inhabitants.

Innocent of the outside world, the Cooks were a regimented missionary kingdom for much of the 19th century. Ancestral power and tradition were often shattered by missionary lawmakers, like the idols and temples in lonely inland groves. The missionaries did their best to provide medical care, but European illnesses such as tuberculosis killed thousands of the sad and bewildered people.

N 1888 the Cooks became a British protectorate, and in 1901 were annexed by New Zealand. Gradually, with better health services, the shadows of the 19th century began to lift, and the population rose again.

Today, though an estimated 11,000 Cook Islanders have chosen urban life in New Zealand, the population is still rising. Those at home—more than 20,000—direct their agriculture to the New Zealand market. In 1965 they elected their own government and chose their first Premier, genial, vigorous Albert Henry. They retain New Zealand citizenship and continue to receive that country's protection and financial support.

Cook Islanders have declined to go along entirely with the 20th century. They have, for example, resisted many of the lures dangled by the world's booming tourist industry. "We're preparing for tourism," the 64-year-old Premier told me, "but we're trying to absorb it gently. Uncontrolled, tourism could swamp us, leaving nothing of the traditional way of life at all—nothing but bitterly disillusioned islanders. We hope that visitors, when they do come, will leave the islands as they found them."

The test of Premier Henry's hope will come in 1973, when jets begin to fly visitors into his islands. Airport construction has already taxed Rarotonga's limited land area; hotel construction is also placing a strain on the island's limited resources. Is it worth it, after all? Will it mean a better life?

"We don't want to lose our identity," islanders insisted to me. There is every reason to hope their wish comes true, for change could only disillusion visitors. Now, with a fast-mounting population of 11,500, Rarotonga is still very much itself—delightfully and colorfully distinct. Nowhere else in Polynesia is the tumultuous tamure danced more electrifyingly. Flowers and song lend the island an air of endless festival.

If ever there was an island of flowers, Rarotonga deserves the name. With the coming of self-government, vigorous village committees began to make parkland of much of the island's shore. And the countless blossoms garland men and women, boys and girls, sometimes even the dogs. Swift fingers fashion hibiscus, frangipani, and the starlike *tiare maori* into necklets and crowns at the slightest excuse, for any occasion.

In surrendering to its Polynesian charm, visitors of the future may have trouble taking this lilliputian state seriously. But that isn't the point: Cook Islanders don't take themselves too seriously either. If they have to make the best of the 20th century, they are determined to make it a happy best.

"It's very difficult, sometimes," young Rarotongan schoolteacher Turepu Turepu confessed to me. "It's so hard to study, to be earnest about the meaning of life, when all around you are people who only want to laugh, dance, sing, and be happy."

And, thus ending the conversation, he began to strum his guitar.

Sunset gilds a wave-lashed reef off Rarotonga, largest of the Cooks, as young anglers with bamboo poles fish for rock cod, parrotfish, mullet, and bream. The group's 15 islands lie scattered over 750,000 square miles of ocean. Captain Cook, whose name they honor, discovered five of them in the 1770's, calling the remote specks "detached parts of the earth."

CHAPTER THREE

SAMOA

The Changed and the Changeless

I HAVE MORE OR LESS the same conversation with Samoan friends every time I visit their ruggedly lovely islands: "Well," I say, hoping to provoke response, "it's good to be back in the thick of Polynesia again."

"Polynesia? You caught the wrong plane. You're in Samoa. These Polynesians you write about, *they* might have come from somewhere else. But we didn't. We come from Samoa."

"Wouldn't you sooner believe your ancestors made those great Pacific voyages?"

"No, we'll leave that to the other Polynesians. We Samoans have always been here, and don't you go forgetting it again!"

With that said, our oversolemn faces can sustain the ritual no longer. We toast the Samoans of Samoa, and then forget the rest of Polynesia.

But early Samoans believed so strongly in their island origin that even the arrival of the Bible with its account of man's beginning in the garden of Eden left them undismayed. For Samoa, of course, *was* the garden of Eden.

In any Samoan conversation you're bound to hear the words *fa'a Samoa*. It means "the Samoan way." As opposed to, say, the *papalagi* — "white man's" — way.

Whirling torches illuminate a cascading waterfall behind David Vaoifi Tusa as he performs his version of an ancient knife dance on the island of Upolu. Fiercely proud of their heritage, Samoans strive to preserve fa'a Samoa—*the Samoan way.*

The word papalagi, or sky-burster, itself tells of the insularity of Samoans. Before the coming of the European, their universe consisted of the islands of Samoa, Tonga, and Fiji. Strangers could come only from beyond the sky. Then one day the sky split where it touched the sea, and an enormous white bird appeared—a sailing ship.

The first sky-bursters arrived with Dutch

Extinct volcanoes provide a playground for Savai'i children and a harbor for Pago Pago, where ships enter a drowned crater. Visitors ride a cable car up Tutuila Island's Mount Alava. Of Samoa's three major islands, Savai'i and Upolu form independent Western Samoa; Tutuila is part of American Samoa.

explorer Jacob Roggeveen in 1722. Nearly 50 years later came the Frenchman Bougainville, and soon many others.

In 1830 came the man Samoans now respect as the literal sky-burster, the true messenger from Heaven. This was the Reverend John Williams of the interdenominational London Missionary Society. The day he landed, the shores of Samoa were dark with the smoke of savage tribal warfare. He could not have brought his message of peace and goodwill to more unpromising islands.

Yet within a few years Christianity had become so much a part of fa'a Samoa that Samoans regarded the outside world as pagan.

"You papalagi never took Christianity seriously," an elderly Samoan once told me. "We

do. You talk about Christianity. We live it."

The Samoan did not sacrifice his traditions to the demands of the new faith. He did not abandon a social system based on the *aiga* — the extended family group of many dozens of relatives closely dependent upon each other. Nor did he discard the pleasantly airy oval thatched-roof house called *fale*.

The papalagi faith did not mean the papalagi way, and today Samoans believe theirs is a land of Christian light in an increasingly godless world. When Pope Paul VI celebrated Mass in Samoa in 1970, while bypassing larger Pacific countries like New Zealand, Samoans did not appear greatly surprised or especially honored. "Naturally the Pope has

to come here," one Samoan churchman announced. "This is God's country."

Only New Zealand's Maoris outnumber this branch of the Polynesian people; Samoans total about 176,300 with perhaps another 30,000 resident in New Zealand and the United States. But in respect for tradition they rank second to none in Polynesia. Even so, change has come, and come fast, to these lush green islands 750 miles west of Tahiti.

"Lovely and lost and half the world away," poet Rupert Brooke once called them. They are lovely still, but only a jet ride away.

And perhaps best of all, there are two of them — two Samoas, fast becoming more and more distinct in character. One is a nation in

its own right, the other linked to the United States. Western Samoa has some 1,130 square miles and 148,560 people. American Samoa has 76 square miles and 27,769 people.

Six years ago I flew by propeller aircraft into Pago Pago, American Samoa. While I waited for customs clearance in the ramshackle shed which served as terminal, a boy shinnied up a tree and tossed down a green coconut for my refreshment. Then a rattling car took me along a dirt road into the quiet town, still recognizably the setting for Somerset Maugham's short story *Rain*. I claimed an antique couch in an old boarding house where barefoot Samoan waitresses with flowers in their hair strummed guitars.

This time, a jet taxied me from the airstrip to a modern terminal shaped like a huge fale. I might have had coffee in the restaurant, and remembered my green coconut with faint regret. Instead I took a new car over smooth tarmac road into town—and to an air-conditioned hotel room with taped music.

The difference was dazing. To reassure myself I took a walk along the shore of Pago Pago's fiordlike harbor. It was this harbor, already in use as a naval station, that prompted the United States to annex the diminutive islands in 1900, making them the only U. S. possession south of the Equator.

Pago Pago was an anomaly, a curiosity, a colorful name, and many Americans had only a vague idea of its location. But in 1961 Idaho-born H. Rex Lee became Governor of American Samoa and determined to make it a showplace. In education he introduced a concept still startling: TV not just as an aid but as a basis for all classroom work.

Some thought television in the South Seas a crazy enterprise. But as a short-term answer to the lack of adequately trained Samoan teachers, the medium swiftly proved its value. Youngsters can begin to comprehend the enormous world beyond their lonely shores via the flickering screen in the classroom.

In the evenings adult-education programs are beamed into Samoan villages between episodes of *Bonanza* and *Gunsmoke*. There is still something utterly incongruous about a big TV set at the center of a traditional fale. But the placid and taciturn Samoan, cross-

Portable television set, atop a broken console, entertains High Chief Vai'ivae and his family in their fale near Pago Pago. Samoan TV broadcasts six evenings a week. Lagoon breezes cool the open-air dwelling; occupants lower mats when it rains.

legged on pandanus matting, has seen papalagi innovations before. These days he even sees astronauts fetched from the sea, right in his backyard, without astonishment. It seems entirely natural to him that men voyaging beyond this planet should return first to Samoa —and, after the bleak wastes of space, receive garlands of the earth's loveliest flowers.

The high-powered U. S. effort to improve education, boost industry, and generally modernize the territory reminds critics of weeding a backyard garden with a bulldozer. But as one administrator emphasized to me, it

helps American Samoans gain the full benefits of Western civilization without emigrating to Hawaii or California. "At the same time," he said, "we're doing our best to keep Samoa for the Samoans."

Responsibility for administering the islands remains with the U. S. Department of the Interior. In the territorial government every voter may cast a ballot for one of 20 Representatives, but chiefs meet in time-honored fashion to select the 18 Senators. In the first territory-wide election, held in 1970, Samoans chose their first delegate-at-large to Washington, High Chief A. U. Fuimaono.

His official role is to present to the Federal Government "the view of the Samoan people." Formerly an educator himself, he wants textbooks—not just TV—in Samoan classrooms, good vocational training, and Samoan

used as the primary language of instruction.

And what of the many Americans who have found their way here? Most of them, teachers and TV technicians and civil servants alike, live in simple homes without air conditioning, reveling in the warm Polynesian climate. A housewife from New Jersey sighed, "It's going to be hard to take winters in the States again. I wasn't too excited about coming here, but now I don't want to leave. And I don't know how I'll ever break the news to the children that we must go back home someday. They've really become Samoan."

From a hill behind the town I took one of the South Pacific's most breathtaking aerial trips—by dizzying cable car swaying along nearly a mile across Pago Pago Harbor. I rode suspended far above docks and town, with bulky peaks crowding around.

Pacific surf thunders against Pyramid Rock, east of Pago Pago, as fishermen head for ho...

ugged 2,142-foot Mount Matafao, American Samoa's highest peak, bulks beyond Pago Pago Harbor.

Redwood ceiling of the Congregational Church of Jesus in Samoa gleams above Sunday worshipers in Pago Pago. Predominantly Protestant, the villages vie to build the most beautiful church. A puletasi-clad mother (above) arrives for the 8 a.m. service with her still-drowsy daughter.

The car stopped on the 1,610-foot summit of Mount Alava, made taller by TV antennas and transmitters. There, in the midst of change, the hum of equipment around me, I looked west across a shiny sea to the island of Upolu, 77 miles away, part of the independent country of Western Samoa.

A DC-3 lifted me across the strip of water that separates the two Samoas, a division perhaps permanent now. American Samoans are unlikely to surrender their link with the United States. Western Samoans, on the other hand, are passionately proud of the independence they achieved in 1962. They regard themselves as true inheritors of fa'a Samoa.

Faleolo Airport was unchanged: a scoria strip, a customs shed. And so was one of the most beautiful drives in the South Pacific, the 20-mile road from Faleolo into Apia town, past lagoon and leaning coconut palm, cathedral-size churches and beehive-like fales grouped about village greens, cricket-playing children and bathing girls in freshwater pools.

Nowhere in Polynesia does tradition announce itself so refreshingly. Tradition is in the bright wraparound skirt, the *lava-lava,* still favored by Samoan men; and in the thatched-roof fale itself, the least-private dwelling in the world, without walls and entirely open to the stranger's gaze. Tradition announces itself in the gentle modesty of Samoan girls, too, the most retiring in Polynesia. They "walk like goddesses," said Rupert Brooke, lamenting his "shattered and fragmentary" heart.

And even the most travel-hardened might echo Brooke in exclaiming, "It's all true about the South Seas!" The serenity of the shore, which brown voyagers claimed before the

time of Christ, left me with the sensation of resuming an old love affair.

When I arrived in Apia, it was certainly the time to resume old friendships. Henry Wendt, my amiable host for a visit in 1961, awaited me beside a laden dinner table.

"Welcome back," he said to me warmly. "I hope you won't find things too different."

A characteristic and progressive business-man of the town, plumber and importer, Henry remains a *matai* — chief — in his home village, elected head of his extended family group. And he returns to his family group frequently to settle disputes, distribute land, and see that no relative is in need.

I once asked Henry if all this wasn't a strain on him. "It's a duty," he said, "but not a duty I have to think about. No more than you, as a papalagi, would think it a duty to love your children. In Samoa the family is everything. We look after our own elderly and sick — it's our kind of social security."

Henry, for all his bland and cheerful sur-face, remains as solidly Samoan as the plate of *palusami* he placed before me. "Cooked for you today," he said, "to give you the taste of Samoa again."

There is really no Pacific food to rival good Samoan palusami, a marvel to the palate and a misery to describe. Basically it is no more than thick coconut cream wrapped in young taro leaf, then baked on hot stones and served on slices of baked taro.

As food diminished, talk expanded. "You see most of my children around me again," Henry said proudly. "And grandchildren too."

Several of Henry's children have gone south to New Zealand for advanced educa-tion and returned. Three of his sons have brought home papalagi wives. One is 31-year-old Albert, who came back with a Master of Arts degree, a thesis on Samoan history, and his attractive schoolteacher wife Jenny. Al-bert is now principal of Samoa College (the equivalent of a U. S. high school).

"It didn't take long to settle back," he told

59

me. "To tune into fa'a Samoa again. I can't imagine living anywhere else in the world."

Next day he took me around his fast-growing hometown. Despite its 30,600 people, Apia is still really a cluster of villages. What holds it together is its waterfront, still South Seas traditional with churches and trading companies. Walk 50 yards from the sea and you might be in an ordinary Samoan village, with fales and families grouped in a neat semicircle around the village green.

From all over the 430 square miles of lumpy Upolu, Apia's busy market summons villagers bearing copra, bananas, and cacao.

But change was pronounced: tourists, taxis, curio shops, nightclubs, a snack bar. A new wharf, the country's first, projected into Apia Harbour; here produce is shipped to New Zealand and Japan. And Apia had surrendered, in the cause of progress, its most notable landmark and link with the past — the rusting wreck of the German gunboat *Adler,* now buried beneath 38 acres of new land created for a town center with fill dredged from a harbor-deepening project.

The *Adler,* with two other warships, stood ready for battle against three American vessels and a British man-of-war in Apia Harbour in 1889. The three powers backed the claims of rival and warring Samoan high chiefs. To Samoans the grave international tension over their islands was clear proof that they were still the true center of the universe.

A hurricane ended the crisis. Roaring out of the Pacific, the storm wrecked three U. S. and three German ships and claimed 150 lives — divine intervention, Samoans believed.

A few years later, Germany took over Western Samoa, only to lose it to New Zealand at the beginning of World War I. New Zealand ruled the islands under the League of Nations and later the United Nations until 1962, when Western Samoa became an independent state. This regained independence would have delighted Robert Louis Stevenson, who involved himself in the cause of Samoan nationalism back in the 1890's.

Stevenson thought the hospitable Samoans, among whom he settled for the last years of his life, the gayest of all Polynesians.

"They are easy, merry and pleasure loving," he wrote. "Song is almost ceaseless." I climbed to his tomb atop 1,148-foot Mount Vaea, following the steep and muddy track hacked by 200 grieving Samoans when they carried the long-roving author to his last resting place in 1894: They styled it "Road of Loving Hearts." Fittingly, Stevenson's old and splendid home at Vailima has become Samoa's equivalent of the White House, residence of the Head of State.

Occasionally one may find a rare royal kava ceremony performed on its wide lawns—like the one I witnessed, four or five years ago, for a distinguished visitor. On each side of the honored guest sat bare-shouldered inheritors of the Samoan royal titles—Fiame Mata'afa, then Prime Minister, and titular Head of State Malietoa Tanumafili II.

In front of them sat an assemblage of the country's matais, chiefs, and their chiefly orators, bearing staffs and fly whisks as symbols of position. For the highest-ranking village chiefs never speak for themselves on any official occasion; the task goes to matais of slightly lesser rank, "talking chiefs" who specialize in Samoan protocol. Thus the rich formal words of farewell were left to a dignified orator. Then, amid chant and dance, the kava bowl was brought forward.

A drink made from the root of the South Pacific pepper plant, *Piper methysticum,* kava is traditionally prepared by a *taupou*—the carefully guarded virgin daughter of a village high chief, a ceremonial princess with headdress of feathers and bleached human hair and a whale-tooth necklace. While the drink was offered to the distinguished guest, I went across the lawn to speak to the plump and cheerful girl who had prepared it.

Niece of Mata'afa, thus of royal blood herself, honey-colored 27-year-old Fa'amusami

Winking television screen holds the attention of students of the Matafao Consolidated School near Pago Pago. Introduced by former Governor H. Rex Lee, the system broadcasts some 190 selections a week on six channels. Transmitters atop Mount Alava beam programs and offer instruction to novice producer-directors (bottom). 61

Lusty Western Samoans, independent since January 1, 1962, welcome an excuse for celebrating. Pulling together, rowers practice for a race in their many-oared fautasi. Drums sound as girls in overskirts of bleached bark perform a war dance. Above, a hatchet-swinging celebrant, clowning for the crowd, flashes a two-toothed grimace. A choir conductor prepares his group for a song of welcome.

White coral sand reflects the midday sun in the village of Falealupo on Savai'i's western tip. Boys in colorful lava-lavas and girls in skirts and blouses — their school uniforms — stroll among palms and relax in the shade during recess.

Ulberg turned out to be one of the few Western Samoan taupous qualified by birth to prepare kava for a royal ceremony. "I was 14 the first time I prepared kava as a taupou," she told me with a smile. "But these days the tradition is a little different."

"In what way?" I asked.

"Well," she laughed, "I still act the taupou — though I'm married and mother of four."

But it was in waterfront government offices, once occupied by pale-skinned New Zealanders, that I found Western Samoan change most impressive. Here I met many old Samoan friends, graduates of New Zealand universities, busy with the future of their tiny new state. One was young government lawyer Herbert Clarke, who took me to meet other civil servants during his kava break — the Samoan equivalent of a coffee break.

"You must understand," Herbert insisted, "that ours will never be a rich country. But it can be a respected one, making its own way in the world — and paying its own way."

It will always be rich for me, in terms of people. Most of my old friends were teaching. But one — Tufuga Efi, son of the late High Chief Tupua Tamasese, who helped guide Western Samoa to independence — had gone into politics to speak for his more sophisticated generation. "Someone has to," he said. "We're no longer a remote, lost place in the middle of the Pacific. On the other hand I don't go overboard for indiscriminate Western-style progress — I want Samoan progress."

In 1970 Western Samoa's leaders were replaced by younger, outward-looking men —

including Tufuga Efi—who now try to persuade a largely self-satisfied society that it can hardly be self-sufficient in future.

Characteristically, Samoans declined to reject tradition in favor of the democratic ideal of universal adult suffrage. Leadership still rests largely in the hands of the country's 9,500 matais, who elect 46 members of the Legislative Assembly. Voting citizens select the other two lawmakers. A Cabinet of nine directs executive matters, but preservation of order is often also in the hands of the chiefs.

I journeyed toward the remotest of those villages when I made a dawn crossing of the 11-mile strait between Upolu and Savai'i.

The old volcanoes of Savai'i, which have shrugged peaks up to 6,000 feet, lay mottled green across pearly water tinted with sunrise. Somewhere in Savai'i's 660 square miles may rest the secrets of Polynesia's origin; secrets still awaiting the archeologist. The very name Savai'i, to me, hints that it was the first Polynesian homeland. To the east Savai'i appears, with dialectical change, as Havai'i, the old name of Raiatea; to the north as Hawaii; in New Zealand it was remembered as Hawaiki, the legendary Maori homeland.

On a previous trip, the old landscape struck me so powerfully that I noted: "I think Samoa has been settled a thousand years longer than anyone guesses—certainly a thousand years before Christ. Why else should they have forgotten so much of their voyaging origin, unlike other Polynesians?"

Now possible evidence had arrived to sustain that conviction. On a high slope of Savai'i I scrambled up an immense stone platform, rising 30 feet in the center of a copra plantation, and until the 1960's hidden by dense overgrowth. The summit of the platform, which I paced out, measured about

65

50 yards by 30. Here and there were stone seats. Plainly for a ceremonial—probably religious—purpose, the platform is recognizably kin to the stone temple platforms of Tahiti, and possibly their forebear.

Savai'i Agricultural Inspector Eddie Ripley, a tough bronze Samoan, told me: "We can't account for it. There's no memory of it, no legend. It doesn't say anything to us."

For me no stones could be more eloquent; here seemed proof of Samoa's antiquity, and a past so old it could be forgotten even by a people who pride themselves on memory.

Perhaps volcano and lava-flow drove many of the original settlers of Savai'i to the sea again. Heading to the west of the island I went through great black lava fields. The last major eruption, between 1905 and 1911, buried much rich land and sent some villagers as refugees to Upolu. Now lonely wildflowers and weeds spring up in cracks in the brittle lava on the abandoned land.

Lava gave way to dense, high forest, to the shore of Asau village, with fales built over the water on volcanic rocks. A few miles inland, the road led through banana plantations and then skirted the coast again. I passed Cape Mulinu'u, Samoa's westernmost tip, which points like an arrow toward Asia; it was in this direction the soul traveled after death, toward the spirit land of Pulotu. But it has always been hard for me to see this palm-tangled cape as the start of what Samoans call "the slippery path, the sliding path of death."

Now it was dusk, and the surf luminous in the fading light. I was near journey's end. The lights and cooking fires of the village of Falelima flickered among fales scattered along the coral sand. The village women and chiefs were waiting, outside the guest fale, to give hospitality to the papalagi stranger.

"Welcome to our village," said the senior chief, gripping my hand, and then leading me into the fale. I sat cross-legged on a mat, my back resting against the post reserved for special guests, and listened with delight to the rich oratory beloved of Samoans. There was food and drink, song and dance.

The changed Samoa I had seen so recently seemed remote—an age away—for now I was in Samoa the changeless.

Samoans, east and west: A smiling trucker and an earnest young churchgoer on Tutuila, a lovely teen-ager from Western Samoa, and two American

Samoans free from school. Among Polynesians, Samoa's increasing population now ranks second only to the Maoris of New Zealand. Below, the Catholic Youth Band from Vaiusu village on Upolu, familiar with both Western musical instruments and Western tunes, musters for a concert.

Framed by a dense growth of fern, Fuipisia Falls plunges 185 feet in the jumbled interior of Upolu; nimble waders venture near the brink. In the lush rain forest, brilliant flowers pierce the gloom. Two varieties of *Heliconia* (1 and 3) conceal blossoms within boat-shaped bracts. Changeable rose-mallow (2), called Confederate rose in southern Florida, blossoms white in the morning hours, changes to pink or red during the day, then dies. Arching plants of torch ginger (4 and 5) may shoot as high as 20 feet. Bright red or pink flower heads spring from leafless stems around the base of the plant. Cultivated for a lei and corsage industry in Hawaii, the hybrid *Vanda Miss Joaquim* (6) first appeared in Singapore in the late 19th century. When introduced in Polynesia, it became known as the Singapore orchid.

DAVID MOORE, BLACK STAR

CHAPTER FOUR

TONGA

The "Friendly Islands" — Polynesia's Last Kingdom

THE OLD SAIL-DRIVEN VOYAGER took days, or even weeks, to make a new landfall among the islands of the South Pacific. But within two hours of departing Samoa our prop-driven DC-3, a sturdy Pacific packhorse, had fetched up first sight of Tonga's seemingly myriad reefs and islands. Out of the hard glitter of an empty ocean they swarmed — streaks of surf and reef, then the glowing green of tiny worlds under a benevolent sun, an exploding bouquet of islands.

Enough islands, one might think, to last any explorer a lifetime.

Yet all 150 of them total only 269 square miles in land area. Scattered to the south of Samoa, the Tongan islands are a Polynesian kingdom the 20th century almost forgot.

Now we winged low over an islet-dappled mosaic of reef and lagoon toward the physical and spiritual heart of that kingdom, the island of Tongatapu. On my lap, as the plane dipped for a landing, lay an 18th-century account of the island by one of Captain Cook's officers: "... neither Hills nor Dales, but a fine continued flat surface, and that, totally cover'd with the various Trees ... so that the prospect is neither more nor less than one compleat Garden ... one of the finest in the World...."

Giant sovereign in velvet and ermine, King Tau-fa'ahau Tupou IV pauses on the veranda of the Royal Palace on the day of his coronation, July 4, 1967. In Tonga great size marks the nobility. The King stands 6 feet 2, weighs 325 pounds.

Coronation day: Exuberant Tongans honor their first new monarch since 1918—the islands' beloved Queen Sālote had ruled 47 years at her death in 1965. Schoolgirls in the finely woven pandanus-leaf ta'ovala—the most distinctive part of Tongan attire —wave their kingdom's flag, a banner bearing the Christian cross in a field of white. A young dancer in a crepe-paper hat flourishes a paddle-shaped club, symbolic of Tonga's warrior past. Royal children bear the King's train; percussionists hammer drums made from oil barrels.

I could have no doubt that, almost two centuries later, I was looking upon the same garden. Cook pronounced Tongans friendly, and, ever since, Tonga has been known as the "Friendly Islands." Tongatapu, with 99 square miles, more than a third of the kingdom in area, has more than three-fifths of its people —by current estimates, some 48,600 of perhaps 81,000 Tongans.

I stepped out of the plane into the balmy Tongan air and met the first of them — smiling customs and immigration officials who waved me swiftly through into a cheerful crowd that greeted returning relatives with fragrant garlands of frangipanis and gardenias. A driver

Tonga's capital, Nuku'alofa lies between ocean and lagoon on the coral island of Tongatapu. Piers reach across a fringing reef to deep water. At sea's edge, the russet cupola of the palace rises behind Norfolk pines; beyond, the Royal Tombs stand on a grassy expanse. The palace guard (opposite) marches before the royal residence.

gathered my bags and sped me 14 miles across the island, through village and plantation, past flowering trees and playing children, to Tonga's seafront capital, Nuku'alofa.

"Since 1967," he told me, "we have begun to have many visitors. Ah, that was a year. Perhaps we will never know one quite like it again. Every Tongan felt taller."

He was recalling, a little wistfully, Tonga's crowning of a new king in 1967, the year Tonga opened its doors to the world for the first time. Friends and dignitaries arrived: from Britain, New Zealand, the United States, Australia, Samoa. And Tongans explained their joy in the coronation, their hope for the future—and unforgotten sorrow for the death of their famous queen, Sālote, a year and a half before.

No Tongan ever forgets he is Tongan, the one Polynesian never under foreign rule; and thus no Tongan ever forgets that his life turns about his monarch, symbol of Tonga's proud independence. Most other Polynesian royal   75

LUIS MARDEN, NATIONAL GEOGRAPHIC STAFF

lines have vanished into obscurity or insignificance. In Tonga royal tradition still triumphs. And it triumphs, moreover, at the very instant that the 20th century hurdles the reef and comes ashore on these sheltered islands. My driver pulled up outside the most pronounced symbol of change—a 50-room luxury hotel, the country's first, finished in 1966 to house coronation guests and then an increasing tourist inflow. Styled the International Dateline Hotel, because of its close

EDWIN STUART GROSVENOR (TOP) AND JACK FIELDS

" 'Tis the season to be jolly...." Tongans in Nuku'alofa tune up for Christmas caroling night, when they serenade visitors to their islands. Music comes easily to Polynesians—most grow up to the lilt of songs, the strum of guitars, the throb of drums. Guitarist Elone Tali (right) performs with a string band that plays on occasion for the King. Below, islanders roast whole pigs—one for each honored guest at a family feast.

77

proximity to the line where each calendar day first dawns, it has now begun to do steady business. The gentle Tongan waiters have become accustomed to their roles.

Other Tongans too have grown used to outsiders. I saw three cruise ships call in five days at Tongatapu, leaving behind some $45,000 with the souvenir vendors, guides, and taxi drivers who crowd the seafront.

Yet, though I wandered in Nuku'alofa in the thick of a noisy rush, I found it still the gentle heart of a gentle kingdom — recognizably still the place Captain Cook saw two centuries ago, with a people "mild and benevolent" who "never appear'd in the smallest degree hostile." The villager who comes to town to sell his tapa or baskets doesn't drive a hard bargain, and can even be quietly apologetic about asking money of a guest in his country.

I found myself treated as an individual, always asked about my country, my family, my religion, my children. A Tongan shopkeeper or souvenir seller seems as eager to make a friend as to make a sale.

When the cruise ships left, Nuku'alofa — which means "the abode of love" — became its quiet self again, a tranquil village of the Victorian era. Within a few yards of each other stand most of the government offices of the kingdom, no more than a two-minute walk from the Royal Palace, a two-story wooden structure, white-walled and red-roofed, with multiple gables, scalloped eaves, and gingerbread trimmings. Neighboring it, among wide lawns and huge rain trees, is the Wesleyan Chapel Royal.

The abode of love, otherwise, seems a blend of Cape Cod and the South Seas — with grass-bordered streets, picket fences, and frame houses among lush tropical gardens. But everywhere, belying the Western atmosphere of the town, are strolling Tongans. Like other Polynesians, Tongans can be happy and easy-going, content with the simplest of pleasures. Their robust build is enhanced by a measured dignity of stance and manner. But to the stranger, Tongans may appear staid in dress by comparison with other Pacific islanders. The black of mourning for deceased relatives is worn for months, so a crowd of Tongans often has a somber hue.

The most distinctive feature of Tongan dress, though, is the ta'ovala — the finely woven pandanus-leaf mat worn around the waist. Without it, particularly on formal occasions, the Tongan feels half-dressed. Often the mats are treasured heirlooms, tattered beyond belief. In 1953, when Queen Sālote Tupou III greeted Britain's visiting Queen Elizabeth II and Prince Philip, she wore a ta'ovala six centuries old.

I traveled back those centuries, and more, as I began to journey about Tongatapu. My first call was on an old friend and fellow New Zealander, bearded and vigorous young archeologist Les Groube. I found him at work six feet down in a carefully excavated pit at the center of the village of Ha'ateiho. I climbed down and shook his hand amid the residue of centuries of Polynesian occupation.

His work on Tongatapu is characteristic of that being done throughout Polynesia. The hunt for clues to end the puzzle of the wandering Polynesians is now gathering impetus. The work of Groube and others like him may make it possible one day for a writer to tell the whole Polynesian story, not just fragments of a do-it-yourself mystery.

"There are so many guesses, so many fairy tales," Les said as his trowel eased away the

Huge sheet of tapa, imprinted with Tonga's coat of arms and bearing allegorical birds and lions, gets careful final highlighting with brush and dye. Sunlight darkens and sets the colors. In decorating tapa, women place the sheets over raised designs stitched to a bark-and-fiber base (detail, left) and rub on stain somewhat as an archeologist takes rubbings from stone inscriptions. To make the thin feltlike sheets, they use ironwood mallets to pound and flatten water-soaked strips of the inner bark of the paper mulberry tree, then join the cloth-like pieces together with manioc-root juice. Tapa finds use in Tonga as clothing, bedding, room dividers, and ceremonial "red carpets."

LUIS MARDEN, NATIONAL GEOGRAPHIC STAFF

MICHAEL E. LONG, NATIONAL GEOGRAPHIC STAFF

Tonga's most abundant natura resource: Young people under 1(account for one-third the island: population of 81,000. At lef schoolgirls leap for a rebouna youngsters (above) race in a down pour. When the brightly cloake boy (opposite) reaches the taxpay ing age of 16, he will be eligibl for some eight acres of land—bu because most plots are taken he ma have to wait many years to clain one. Robust health brightens th face of a young girl; all Tongan get free medical care. A boy swing on a rusting airstrip panel lef from World War II, when Tong, served as an Allied staging area

earth gripping a stone adz. "But I only know one sure way to get at the facts about the Polynesian—about how and why he settled the South Pacific. That's to unearth clues like this by careful excavation."

The word "tonga" actually means "south" in many Polynesian languages; thus I had always supposed Tongatapu to mean "sacred south." That is, until I met the plump and genial Tongan nobleman the Honorable Ve'ehala, Governor of Ha'apai. One of the kingdom's 33 hereditary nobles, Ve'ehala formerly served as Keeper of the Palace Records, helping preserve Tongan traditions as one of the duties of his office.

"Actually," he said, "in the Samoan language, 'tonga' can also mean 'garden.' Our first monarch, the tenth-century Tu'i Tonga, was thus, in literal meaning, 'king of the garden.' So Tongatapu, where the kings lived and died,

JACK FIELDS (ABOVE AND RIGHT)

EDWIN STUART GROSVENOR   MICHAEL E. LONG, NATIONAL GEOGRAPHIC STAFF

means 'sacred garden.' Later—much later— the meaning of the word, here and elsewhere in Polynesia, may have evolved into 'south,' because Tonga was in fact in the south."

The name "sacred garden" seems to fit the kingdom perfectly. Or so I feel when I look at Tonga today. Everywhere a hallowed past mingles with the present.

One reminder of antiquity is the mighty *Ha'amonga,* two upright pillars of coral bear-

ing a massive lintel estimated to weigh more than nine tons. Tradition says the trilithon, standing eerily alone in the countryside, was built seven centuries ago as a monument for the sons of King Tu'itātui. Tonga's present King believes it may have served as a device for determining the seasons. He found that grooves in the structure pointed eastward, and had a path cleared of vegetation in line with one of them to see if it would indicate

81

the point of sunrise at the solstices. A sign at the site describes the result of his experiment: "On June 21st 1967 at dawn [the winter solstice in the Southern Hemisphere] His Majesty was present at this place and it was a thrilling moment when the sun rose at the exact point indicated by his interpretation of the lines etched on the great stone.... it is now clear how it was used to determine the season in ancient times."

Not far from the trilithon I saw the sacred flying foxes of Kolovai. Hundreds upon hundreds of these chattering fruit bats hang head down in a grove of trees at the village center.

"They were given to a great Tongan navigator by his beloved, a Samoan princess, perhaps four centuries ago," an aging villager told me. "He brought them to Kolovai, where they roosted and have remained ever since as a symbol of that woman's love."

Centuries-old rituals also still persist. Outside a Nuku'alofa office I saw a citizen approach a noble; the man sank to the ground, crossing his legs and making his two hands into a single fist. Then he spoke his piece to the noble. His attitude, traditionally, placed him at the mercy of the man standing.

"One feels no abasement in the act," a Tongan friend explained cheerfully. "Out of such rituals has Tonga survived. It is our way, and our strength. When a man performs such an act, he is just being Tongan."

In the old state religion of Tonga, it was held that only king and aristocrat possessed an afterlife; the commoner had none, and even his life upon this earth was believed of little value. Tongans, though they seemed

friendly to Cook and his men, were fierce warriors, frequently involved in the wars of nearby Fiji. In the 13th century, Tongans even held in thrall their more numerous Samoan cousins. Their great double canoes, laden with warriors, could spread terror throughout neighboring islands.

In parts of Polynesia, the arrival of Christianity weakened old authority. Here it gave new substance to such authority. An early convert, in 1831, was High Chief Taufa'ahau, who in a series of wars united Tonga and lent his support to the Wesleyan Methodist missionaries. In 1845 he emerged as King George Tupou I. Thirty years after beginning his reign he introduced constitutional government.

He died in his 97th year, head of a unified and Christian Tonga, where commoners now possessed souls. Liberated from serfdom they could also possess land. King George instituted a scheme unique in the Pacific that made it possible for every Tongan man to apply for some eight acres of land on attaining the taxpaying age of 16 years.

During the reign of his great-grandson George II (1893-1918), the independent kingdom placed itself under the protection of Great Britain. In 1918 the beloved Queen Sālote, a magnificent figure of Tongan royalty six feet two inches tall, began her long reign.

A large-hearted woman from a microscopic land, she won the affection of millions in Britain when she rode bareheaded and smiling in an open carriage through the chill rain of London to the coronation of Elizabeth II on June 2, 1953. Fond of the motto "Tonga's mountain is in its heart," she seemed by the

Driven by wind and tide, surf plumes from blowholes in the coral coast of Tongatapu. Hundreds of openings, large and small, pierce the rocky ledge on the windward side. When water surges through the vents, this shore appears fringed with geysers. Though a few such blowholes occur on other islands, none spout more spectacularly than those of Tongatapu — one giant fountains as high as a hundred feet.

Spotted pebble crab, hunted at night by fishermen with gasoline lanterns or coconut-sheath torches, ambles sluggishly along offshore reefs. Island shallows also abound with turtles, clams, squid, and fish.

LUIS MARDEN (LEFT) AND MICHAEL E. LONG, BOTH NATIONAL GEOGRAPHIC STAFF

time of her death in 1965 an enduring mountain in the Polynesian scene.

She had gently protected her people from the temptations of an increasingly sophisticated Pacific. Nowhere else in Polynesia has the stern puritan spirit of the missionaries persisted longer. Tongan men dare not go without shirts in public, at risk of fine and censure; most girls swim in their dresses. The law enforces respect for the Sabbath.

"Sure I'll take you fishing," a Tongan friend told me, "but not on Sunday. That might mean a ten-dollar fine or three months in jail at hard labor." He showed me Tonga's Constitution and there it was: "The Sabbath Day shall be sacred in Tonga forever and it shall not be lawful to do work or play games or trade on the Sabbath...."

Sālote had, in fact, left Tonga an innocent idyll in the 20th century. Can such an idyll endure? Unlike other Polynesian territories, Tonga has no official migration outlets to relieve population pressure; perhaps only a few more than 1,000 live away from home, mostly in New Zealand. "Samoans can emigrate to the United States or New Zealand," a young Tongan said to me sadly. "Cook Islanders can go to New Zealand, Tahitians to France. We can go elsewhere only with difficulty. That's the price of our Pacific independence."

Today on the average there are at least 300 Tongans to every square mile, putting the kingdom among the South Pacific's most crowded islands; on Tongatapu the figure exceeds 480. And the kingdom has little but agriculture as resource. Copra and bananas are the main exports.

Tongans remain close to the soil. My taxi

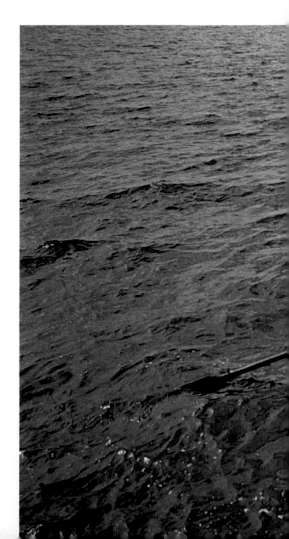

Captain David Fifita (above) sits in the stern of Malolelei, *a makeshift outrigger he and 16 other shipwrecked Tongans built on desolate Minerva Reef in 1962 with only a hammer, knife, and 6-inch spike. Following a course he scratched on a plank, Fifita, his son, and a crewman sailed 450 miles to Fiji. Their boat overturned in sight of land, and the son drowned trying to swim to shore. Fifita and the crewman survived and sent rescuers to their waiting compatriots. By the end of the 14-week ordeal, four men had died on the reef. The others, sheltered in the hull of a wrecked Japanese trawler, lived on fish and fresh water condensed from the sea with an oil-drum still.*

driver worked his eight acres on his days off, planting bananas for the New Zealand market or gathering coconuts for copra. So did the photographer who took my visa portrait, and the waiter at the hotel. "Without land a Tongan is nothing," they would tell me.

Yet land has become scarce—I met middle-aged men still waiting for their eight acres. The lot of many landless Tongans is poverty in a land of fruitful beauty. The idyll is clearly over. Tonga now seeks new ways for survival through expansion of fisheries, increased cattle and coconut production, village handicrafts—and tourism.

How much will Tonga change now? Its intelligent islanders will no doubt draw sharp contrasts with the outside world. Some may well grow restive under a feudal and paternal system of government. It is impossible to overlook contrasts between the lot of the nobility—33 men who owe their power to right of birth—and the lot of the commoner. If commoners now have souls, they also have a right to a better life on earth: a life of value.

In 1971 the kingdom was shaken by its first strike ever—of government nurses against hospital conditions and pay. If some citizens were shocked, others pointed out that women were standing up for their rights. At least one Tongan expected further strikes in future "because one cannot turn back the clock and progress is progressive."

Yet the characteristic older Tongan hopes to see no change at all in his lifetime. "To change would be to show lack of faith in God," one told me. "God will look after us."

Undoubtedly, whatever happens, the ordinary Tongan will not change much. On the whole, he will remain patient gardener and intrepid fisherman. In August and September, when migrating sperm and humpback whales appear offshore, Tongan men in open boats will still prove themselves masters of the sea as they ride down upon their quarry. For here the whale is hunted with harpoon launched by hand—from small speeding craft

under full sail. Tongans hunt not for the oil, but for the meat; not a digestible scrap of the great mammals goes to waste.

And even if Tongatapu changes, the rest of the kingdom — 35 other inhabited islands — will likely go its old quiet way, as remote from the 20th century as ever. In the Ha'apai Group north of Tongatapu, some islands barely peek above the sea, while one, Kao, spires 3,380 feet. Farther north still is the spectacular Vava'u Group. Here the voyager makes his way up a seven-mile channel, past coral heads and volcanic islands rising sheer on either side, to the group's tiny capital of Neiafu, where neat houses dot the hillside.

TO THE TONGAN the Sabbath will always remain truly special, a day to hymn the Creator with dignity and splendor, and, almost as important, a day to feast. Young Pupunga Mahe, whom I met working as assistant at Les Groube's archeological site, invited me to his family's feast, after church service.

Pupunga's home village, like most on Tongatapu, is now a mixture of styles, thatched roofs here, corrugated-iron rooftops there. Also like most Tongan villages, it stands amid small plantings of paper mulberry trees.

Women with wooden mallets and supreme patience lightly pound strips of the inner bark of the paper mulberry into tapa, intricately patterned material once worn by all Tongans and now reserved for ceremonial dress.

When I arrived for the feast, I was greeted with the ceremonial kava cup and guided to a casual lean-to of coconut matting, built to shade the guests. Food was placed on a mat resting on grass, around which we sat cross-legged. If a simple mat could groan, this one would have; there are no half-measures about Tongan hospitality. It would be discourteous to offer a guest a portion of a pig, or even half a pig; he must be given the *whole* pig, to select the portion he prefers. Whole pigs, whole chickens, whole fish, whole crabs — all fresh from the earth oven, along with yams the size of a human leg, and delicacies from sea and land cooked with coconut milk in taro leaf. I did my best, but made faint impression on the immense quantities of food set before me. The waste seemed appalling.

"Waste?" laughed Pupunga. "There's never waste in a Tongan feast. You see."

When we rose, an avalanche of less senior members of the family descended on the food. After them came still a third sitting. Domestic animals got scraps and bones.

Pupunga and I talked while the feast was demolished. Like other young Tongans who now feel trapped by the political boundaries that have sprung up through the ocean their ancestors roamed without restriction, he yearns to travel. Some young men follow in the footsteps of their fighting forefathers, boxing professionally around the world.

But not Pupunga — he told me he would rather pick up a trade in New Zealand and bring his new skills home to Tonga. "I'm sure I really couldn't be happy anywhere else," he confided. "I'm loyal to Tonga."

Loyalty — a word I heard everywhere, the common denominator of the Tongan. The word is uttered as much by the young and university-educated who have returned from distant lands as by the old and staid who have never left their cherished islands.

For on that last and unforgettable coronation day in 1967 there were no generations. There were simply Tongans. Tongans showing their loyalty not just to their new sovereign but to their enduring Polynesian nation.

On that day a smiling giant in ermine-trimmed red velvet robes, King Taufa'ahau Tupou IV, then 49 years old, received tribute from his subjects, and from most of the South Pacific. As songs soared and hundreds of barefoot dancers hammered the tropical earth, Tonga slipped another link into its long tradition. The King, through his mother, Queen Sālote, can trace his ancestry back a thousand years to the first Tu'i Tonga.

And as the new monarch accepted the lusty acclaim of his people, I remembered the quiet words of a young, university-educated Tongan: "To be a Tongan," he explained, "is to be a sentimentalist."

Emerald oases of Vava'u, Tonga's northernmost island group, stretch toward the horizon across a velvet sea. Encircling reefs cup pale green lagoons. Of the 34 isles of Vava'u — most of them high and densely forested — 21 remain uninhabited.

MICHAEL E. LONG, NATIONAL GEOGRAPHIC S

CHAPTER FIVE

NEW ZEALAND

The Long Bright World

"AND WHY are you going to live in New Zealand?" I asked.

"A better life, maybe," said the young Tongan boy. "Anyway better money."

"Just for jobs," said one of the two Samoan boys. "New Zealand is a paradise for jobs, and Samoa is getting crowded."

"All my family will be leaving for New Zealand," said the young man from the remote Tokelau atolls, "because there's nothing back home for us—just sand and coconut trees. Education's hard to get, and I want to learn a trade."

At Nandi International Airport in Fiji, the crossroad of the South Pacific, I sat talking to four young Polynesian islanders while we waited for a jet to speed us 1,148 miles south to Auckland, New Zealand. Each was aiming at permanent residence. And in each was sadness and confidence—sadness at leaving his tropical islands, confidence in winning his way in a new and very different world.

Giant jet might have replaced giant ocean-going canoe, but these young men were clearly inheritors of tradition. The old voyagers followed stars to New Zealand; these new migrants fly at 38,000 feet, guided by radio signals. The old voyagers in their swift sail-

Tattooed Maori chief gazes from the carved stern-post of a war canoe that carried 100 warriors. When Maori Polynesians built the craft 135 years ago, they dominated New Zealand. Now they total fewer than 8 percent of its people.

N.G.S. PHOTOGRAPHER JAMES L. AMOS (ABOVE); DAVID MOORE, BLACK STAR (UPPER RIGHT); MICHAEL E. LONG, N.G.S. STAFF

and-paddle canoes might have taken as little as three weeks, or more than a month; these migrants make the journey in hours.

This new wave of Polynesian migration to New Zealand began soon after World War II and now totals over 30,000. The first migration, more than a thousand years ago, is lost in the silences of Pacific prehistory and may have numbered no more than a hundred.

Consider what New Zealand must have meant to those first Polynesians. They might have been lost fishermen from Rarotonga or Raiatea, carried by winds and currents some 2,000 miles southwest into cool latitudes. They might have been refugees leaving an overpopulated island or in blind flight from tribal warfare or religious feud. Or they may have been adventurous young gamblers,

playing the Polynesian lottery of islands.

There was the incredible size of this new empty land, for one thing. Two main islands, separated by a narrow strait, stretch almost a thousand miles, north to south, and hold 102,374 square miles of land—ten times the rest of Polynesia's isles combined. The shore must have seemed endless to men from tiny tropical island and atoll. The Polynesians

Sprawling Auckland, greatest urban center of Polynesia, spreads beyond its isthmus boundaries. Maoris shaped its volcanic cones into huge fortresses; now high-rise buildings mark the skyline near Waitemata Harbour. In the city's subtropical climate, a palm frames the massive sculpture of a Maori tribesman, his kaitaka *(flaxen cloak) stylized in bronze, and a shopper carries her umbrella against passing showers of early spring.*

91

called their new home *Aotearoa,* which can be interpreted as "long, bright world." For this country was more than islands: to them it *was* a world, huge and dazzling, perhaps terrifying in the immensity of its wonders.

There were strange white mountains, beyond belief in height and number—more than 220 of them soaring above 7,500 feet. There were earthquakes, living volcanoes, geysers, places where the earth itself boiled. There were immense forests, tall and tangled, low and ferny, sometimes ablaze with flowering trees. There were the birds, wayward creatures of evolution, many fantastically flightless in the absence of animal predators.

And more yet, wherever they moved—

beaches as long as 50 miles; vast shiny lakes to mirror man and snow-capped mountain; glaciers swooping thousands of feet down almost to the sea, crumbling noisily in the summer heat; and cold fiords of primeval quiet. This was far from the Polynesia of limpid lagoon and coconut palm. This was a land of challenge, a land in the grand manner.

They endured, they adapted, they built, and they multiplied. At the time of Captain Cook's arrival in 1769, they may have numbered as many as a quarter of a million. The descendants of the voyagers came to call themselves Maoris—from their term *tangata maori,* "man native to the place." In New Zealand the Polynesian had found a home-

Spinnakers full, 5.5-meter sailboats race in Waitemata Harbour. North Islanders, all within two hours of mild seas, can boat the year around; Auckland's summer regatta, held each January, draws one of the world's great gatherings of yachts. At left, hiking crewmen hold a dinghy on its feet.

land worthy of his aspirations, large enough to contain his robust and restless soul. Here he excelled in war and oratory; here his arts, especially carving, found perfection.

Tiritiri o te Moana, an early Polynesian name for New Zealand, can translate as "the gift of the sea." This was not only a gift from the Pacific for the Polynesian; it was also to become a Pacific frontier for the British.

My DC-8 dipped for a landing at Auckland's international airport. Now the Polynesia of small green islands seemed dissolved entirely. Far below sprawled a modern city — highway and freeway, suburb and urban complex, industry and docks — set on a slender isthmus between two great harbors. To north and south stretched farm country, greenly cushioning the explosion of human energy that has made this city of 625,000 people, and that makes New Zealand seem, at times, a patch of Europe in the South Seas.

It was difficult even for me, looking down upon my home city, to believe that just 130 years ago Auckland was no more than a frontier post, a few tents and huts along a scrub-by foreshore. By a treaty signed in 1840 a British official claimed New Zealand for Victoria, Queen of England, and called the almost uninhabited isthmus its capital. And Europeans began to settle under the fifty extinct volcanic cones that dotted the region — cones the Maoris had shaped, over centuries, into the largest prehistoric fortresses known to modern man; the earthworks remain dramatic upon the horizon to this day.

It was always a land for the adventurous to claim, and the British adventure was to be as dramatic as the Polynesian. To journey in New Zealand today is to journey through living adventure, and see a new and unique Pacific nation in the making. For just as the

DAVID MOORE, BLACK STAR; PAINTING ABOVE, "CHIEF TE AHO O TE RANGI, NGATI-MAHUTA TRIBE," BY C. F. GOLDIE, O.B.E., AUCKLAND INSTITUTE AND MUSEUM, COURTESY MRS. C. F. GO

Hei tiki, *a contorted human figure of New Zealand jade, has become the most widely known symbol of Maori art. In the 1916 painting at center, a tribal chief wears a similar ornament and jade ear pendants. His tattooed face bears designs like those on the village gate guard at left, a wood carving believed to predate Cook's arrival in 1769. For prestige, Polynesians paid tattoo artists to cut or puncture the skin and rub in soot.*

Polynesians took leave of warm dreamy islands to make new lives in the large southern land, so men and women voyaged from the comfort of Britain to make for themselves a new destiny far to the south of Asia.

Busy, booming Auckland is one result of the adventure—no longer capital, but by far the country's largest city, with a third of its industry and trade, and a fifth of the nation's 2.9 million people. A maritime, salty-flavored city of coves, bays, and beaches, Auckland has risen beside an island-sprinkled gulf. Ask any Aucklander—and I'm one—how he spends his leisure and chances are he'll say he yachts, or fishes. For often he's as much a man of the sea as the Polynesian before him.

And he enjoys an amiable in-between climate that allows tropical fruit to ripen beside apples, peaches, and plums. Vineyards color the city's western fringe.

It was good to get my feet on native ground again and stroll up Auckland's main thoroughfare, Queen Street. From the docks at the foot of the street cranes swung butter, cheese, wool, and frozen meat aboard cargo ships for shipment to Britain, Australia, Europe, Asia, and the United States. No matter how large its urban centers grow, this South Pacific nation's prosperity still depends on the impressive efficiency of its farmers.

I left the racket of the docks for the jingling bustle of commerce. Fast-changing Auckland always has some surprise for me after a trip away: old landmarks felled, new buildings pushing the skyline higher. One of the city's most splendid recent acquisitions is a tall and magnificently dignified bronze sculpture of a Maori near the foot of Queen Street. Sixty years earlier colonial Aucklanders would have preferred a statue honoring some distant British monarch. But today, increasingly sophisticated, no longer a quaint

Maori war canoe 135 years old and 82 feet long intrigues visitors in the Auckland Institute and Museum. Carvers chiseled openwork spirals on tall sternposts and created designs on timbers of meetinghouses and storehouses like the 19th-century structures reassembled in the museum's Maori Court. Stylized human figures in wood stood atop houses and beside village entrances.

95

Scalding-hot caldron, Frying Pan Lake seethes and bubbles with sulphurous gas. Many such basins on North Island's Volcanic Plateau hold water heated by steam from boiling rivulets thousands of feet below. Through fissures in the faulted rock, and through holes drilled to harness the thermal energy to generators, hot vapors and water rush to the surface. Karapiti Blowhole (opposite), most spectacular of the steam vents, reddens with sparks and flame after a guide thrusts a burning sack into the jet.

DAVID MOORE, BLACK STAR

outpost with its eyes fixed on Great Britain as "home," Auckland takes genuine pride in its Polynesian inheritance.

That inheritance is more than just symbolic. For a century Auckland was almost totally British. But after 1945 New Zealand's exploding Maori population began shifting from country to city in thousands, seeking new livelihood in industry, on the docks, in transport services. And from the tropics came other Polynesians, in hundreds and then thousands, seeking opportunity their tiny island homelands could never give them.

So now Auckland has become the urban center of Polynesia. More than 20 Polynesian languages and dialects are spoken in the city. Within its central area is the greatest concentration of Polynesians in the South Pacific.

But diverse, cosmopolitan Auckland isn't the whole of New Zealand. Nor are the country's two great land masses of North Island and South Island. At the southern tip, pointing toward Antarctica, lies diminutive Stewart Island, famed for its oysters and its scenery. To get my entire country again in perspective, I began by traveling up the subtropical neck of North Island to the Bay of Islands, where long rugged limbs of land nurse a galaxy of green isles. Cook named the place after anchoring here in 1769 and pronouncing it blessed with "every kind of

DAVID MOORE, BLACK STAR

Sole survivor of an order of beak-headed reptiles that flourished in the age of dinosaurs, the soft-spiked tuatara — about two feet long — inhabits islands off New Zealand. It requires 20 years to reach maturity and lives more than a century.

refreshments." French explorers, who arrived three years later, called it Treachery Bay after seemingly friendly Maoris killed and ate their leader, Marc-Joseph Marion du Fresne. But Cook's verdict endured — the whalers from Nantucket and Plymouth who began calling here at the start of the 19th century indeed found every kind of refreshment: Grog shops roared along the shore. Missionaries followed right behind.

I drove to the town of Waitangi beside the bright bay — to virtually hallowed ground for all New Zealanders. Here on February 6, 1840, Maori tribal chiefs under missionary influence ceded their sovereignty over Aotearoa to the British Crown and gave the Queen's government sole right to purchase their lands. In return the Maoris received guarantees of law and order and protection from land speculators, for British settlers had begun to arrive in surging number.

It was February 6 again, now New Zealand's national day. Hundreds of vehicles clogged the narrow route up to a small white wooden building, New Zealand's first British residency. On its wide lawns the Treaty of Waitangi was accepted by dignified Maori chiefs 131 years before. This document was remarkable in the history of European colonization — for the first time a native people was approached as equal. And its spirit was never entirely lost, despite later racial conflicts in which the Maoris lost much cherished tribal land. New Zealand's Maoris are today the Pacific's most prosperous Polynesians, and by far the best educated — with doctors, anthropologists, journalists, diplomats.

A country of many modest successes in social legislation, New Zealand is seen at its best in racial policy. Intermarriage is to me the final test of good race relations, and in New Zealand the rate is high. Among friends and close acquaintances I can count a dozen mixed marriages, happy and successful.

Thousands of other New Zealanders,

brown and white, mingled beside the sunlit waters of the bay, where anchored ships of the Royal New Zealand Navy boomed salute with their guns. Independent of Britain politically, an entirely self-governing dominion since 1907, New Zealand celebrates February 6 not for any colonial association but for the meeting and blending of Europe and Polynesia. Together in solemn ceremony, New Zealanders of two races prayed that we should be "knit together as one people."

That phrase has growing significance. From its low point of 42,000 people near the turn of the century, after tribes had been reduced by European disease and musket warfare, the healthy Maori race has soared to 225,000. With increasing intermarriage, more than one-fourth of all New Zealanders may have

some Polynesian blood by the year 2000.

I flew south, above the wide, rich pastureland along the Waikato River, then the volcano-blasted heartland of North Island, and over the capital city of Wellington.

Each district has its own story. The Waikato territory, much of it taken from Maoris in the warfare of the 1860's, is boasted as having one of the world's greatest concentrations of dairy herds. The Volcanic Plateau, where mountains smoke and geysers spray, is a paradise of trout-rich lakes set amid immense pine forests. And Wellington, made capital in 1865 because of its central location at the southern tip of North Island, is the place where the world's first modern welfare state took shape, beginning in the 1890's.

Ahead of my plane rose the mighty peaks

of South Island. I was intent on leaving urban New Zealand behind, even historic New Zealand. In my race to the cold southern tip of the Polynesian triangle, before winter set in, I was heading for New Zealand primeval.

When my plane touched down in Christchurch, I felt the cold breath of the Pacific south. And I watched a U. S. plane climb into the sky for the 1,400-mile hop to Antarctica. Now rear base for American and New Zealand Antarctic endeavor, Christchurch has an English provincial charm, with cathedral square and willow-hung river.

Christchurch indeed often constitutes the conventional outside view of New Zealand: a "little Britain" of the South Seas. Yet in truth the city is a relic of an older, colonial New Zealand; these spires and genteel gardens have little to do with the experience of the modern New Zealander. No longer simply a brimming food-basket for Britain, New Zealand is fast learning to go it alone in the Pacific, boosting industry and expanding new trade with Japan and the United States. Nation-making was accelerated by British moves toward merger with continental Europe in 1971. The message rings clear: New Zealanders must make do with themselves. And that, in this glowing green frontier land, is a task with many compensations.

Driving across the wide Canterbury Plains, crop-quilted and grazed by fattening lambs, I felt I was traveling a continent. Ahead grew the Southern Alps. This long mountain spine of South Island rises to its greatest height in 12,349-foot Mount Cook, called Aorangi,

Like rhinestones and rubies in a royal setting, the lights of Wellington blaze at dusk around deep Lambton Harbour and on the slopes of the encircling hills. Capital of New Zealand, the city still displays the British coat of arms on a government building constructed in colonial days.

"cloud piercer," by the Polynesian, an echo of Tahiti's Mount Aora'i, and today a thrilling test for mountaineer and skier. Hard against these peaks of everlasting snow, among tussock foothills, are the great sheep and cattle stations of New Zealand, many of 10,000 acres, one of nearly 500,000 acres.

I spent a night on such a station as guest of author-sheepman David McLeod, in one of the oldest surviving homesteads of the South

Island's high country. While frost and night meshed thick on the mountains, a warm log fire glowed within the century-old walls as we talked. Years earlier David, a tranquil philosopher, had told me: "The peace of mind one can find in the mountains is like no other." I could see that peace of mind as he spoke with loving concern of his challenging environment. "This high country, of course, was cleared long before the Europeans came," he said. "Now it's thought the first Polynesians destroyed the forest—burning it off perhaps in the hunt for the moa."

The giant moa, which grew as tall as an African elephant, was the most fabulous of all New Zealand's flightless birds; it was hunted for food, and finally became extinct before Europeans arrived in New Zealand. Over the plains and valleys that were once its haunt, livestock now graze in astonishing numbers: New Zealand counts 60 million sheep and 8.2 million cattle.

Next day I crossed a narrow, winding pass through the Alps and then plunged 3,000 feet to South Island's west coast. Thinly settled by the Maoris, this coastal strip, between mountain and roaring surf, was purchased by the British for a mere 300 gold pieces in 1860, a sum soon to be returned thousandsfold. For just as the Polynesian found this rainy, densely forested region rich in jade for ornament and weapon, the European found its riverbeds spectacularly rich in alluvial gold. Gold-seekers from all over the Pacific rushed the shore. A century later once-prosperous communities have shrunk or vanished. Coal is mined, timber felled, but the precious metal is gone.

It was this shore that Dutch explorer Abel Tasman sighted in December, 1642, imagining it the limb of a continent. A brief and bloody clash with Maoris deterred him

DR. ALFRED M. BAILEY (FAR LEFT), DR. M. F. SOPER (TOP), DAVID MOORE, BLACK STAR (MIDDLE), AND R. J. GRIFFITH

Soaring gannets approach breeding grounds in New Zealand after a 1,000-mile flight from Australia. A red-tailed tropic bird hurries to its nesting place in the outlying Kermadec Islands. Found only in New Zealand, the flightless kiwi has become the national emblem. A pair of red-billed gulls nest in a rocky coastal crevice.

103

Benmore Dam and its power station on the Wai-taki River convert glacial melt from the distant Southern Alps into electricity for New Zealanders on both North and South Islands. Six great concrete tubes, or penstocks (left center; detail, right), funnel water from the lake to turbines below.

from landing, but his voyage was to leave the name Nieuw Zeeland beside a shaky, mysterious line on the world's maps.

The coast road took me through thick, creepered rain forest. About 100 miles farther south, two great glaciers in the Mount Cook region — the Fox and the Franz Josef — inched through fern near the sea, announcing that I was in the cold south of Polynesia. Lakes threw up reflections of snow-tipped mountains; the forest had profound hush. Then, as often happens on this blustery coast, the sky seemed to burst. My car floundered through floodwater and bucked to a stop. I was stranded for two days, my way blocked ahead and behind, before I resumed my journey along a lonely road garlanded by high waterfalls.

Finally I turned east and crossed the Southern Alps, leaving rain and evergreen forest for the arid and sunlit hills of the Province of Otago, settled by Scots in the 1850's and rich in autumn colors. European trees planted by sheepman and gold-seeker brighten lakeside and river flat.

At its east-coast rim, Otago has the misty, hilly city of Dunedin, proud of its Scottish origin. The bagpipes are still often heard here. And a statue of poet Robert Burns sits in the city's octagonal heart, among streets named for distant Edinburgh. Burns, whose nephew Thomas helped found the city, is celebrated too in the name of a literary fellowship awarded annually by Dunedin's Otago University, oldest in the country.

One Dunedin-born inheritor of Burns' bardic voice is 44-year-old James K. Baxter, a poet who has sung more truly and gracefully of his native islands than anyone else of his generation. In his verse the myths of Polynesia blend with the legends of Greece. Of Scots-English descent, he is married to a Maori, a skillful writer herself; their children reflect the increasing mixture of races here. "I

suppose this country will always be a pain and a joy to me," he has told me. "For me it is like a lover or wife. On the one hand, domesticated and respectable — on the other the face of a primeval goddess pitted by the sun, by earthquake and the waves of the sea."

I turned back toward that primeval goddess when I left Dunedin. Among blunt hills and glacier-scoured lakeland, past roaring river and precipitous bluff, my journey took me far from the autumn blaze of Europe's trees, far from cities, far from the works of man. Before me awaited the stark evergreen forest, lofty waterfalls and loftier peaks of Fiordland. This terrain of immense, deeply ice-dissected rocks has, with glacial retreat, been invaded by water — in the west by sea, in the east by melted snows behind natural dams of morainic debris.

But I'd come for more than landscape. It was in Fiordland, during a five-week stay in 1773, that Captain Cook befriended the most southern men he saw in Polynesia. At the lakeside township of Te Anau, on the fringe of Fiordland, I left tourist-beaten tracks and boarded a floatplane to fly in to the remote, wild, and now uninhabited sound where Cook and his men made camp.

Flying here is a precarious business even in the best weather. "Sometimes we can't get down there for weeks at a time," Pilot Ken Leahy told me. We took fishing lines and food in case cloud or storm should shut us off from civilization and made last-minute checks of the weather *(Continued on page 111)*

Luminous spring clouds drift among snowy pinnacles of the Southern Alps. Mount D'Archiac, at right, rears 9,279 feet.

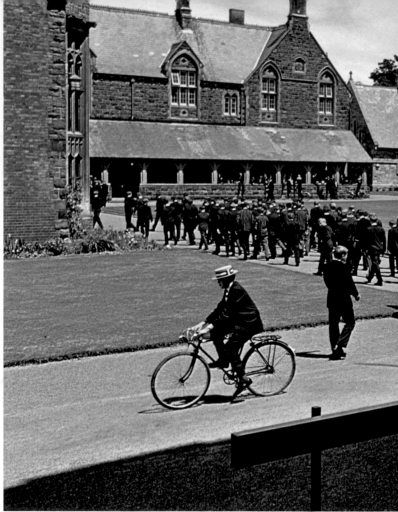

Jauntily dressed teen-ager in downtown Christchurch reflects the city's English heritage and tastes as much as boys in blazers (above) at Christ's College, an exclusive secondary school a few blocks away. The great-grandfathers of many young people in South Island's largest urban center began arriving in 1850 to start a planned community at the seaside edge of the

Canterbury Plains. Organized by the Church of England and carefully chosen from all social classes and a variety of occupations, the settlers created in New Zealand a bit of England.

Boys in standard Christ's College attire stroll to the dining room in one of the Victorian Gothic buildings on the Quadrangle. Commuters (lower left) board a bus bound for suburban Papanui.

Just off the central square, a sprightly girl (far right) walks near the lofty Gothic spire of Christchurch Cathedral. Schoolgirls in uniform snap pictures on the grounds of the church. The more-English-than-England aspect of the city often surprises visitors.

Sheep — 60 million of them — supply wool and meat, New Zealand's main exports, for a world-wide market. At shearing time on a Te Anau farm east of Fiordland's mountains, Bruce McKenzie separates a bleating lamb from the flock.

we might strike. The morning mists were burning off under the sun as we took off.

Lakes unwound beneath, long limbs of water clasping verdant heights. We passed over our last sight of man's handiwork: a large new hydroelectric project harnessing Fiordland waters for the island's growing aluminum industry. Soon it became an insignificant graze upon the pristine splendor of the country. We picked our way bumpily among cloud and peak — up to 5,000 feet and more on each side — and sheer rock faces shiny with melting frost. To the east stretched evergreen forest and high lonely lakes, to the west silver fiords and surf-creamed islands. And everywhere waterfalls gleamed, in thundering tumult or trembling tangle.

Ahead, bulky with islands and serene under low cloud, was the fiord Cook called Dusky Bay, mapped today as Dusky Sound. "No country on earth," he wrote, "can appear with a more rug[g]ed and barren aspect." For him, as now for me, this was the end of Polynesia. Our floats carved water into a cove.

Looking about, Ken became concerned about the weather. "We can't stay if this cloud thickens," he announced as we taxied.

For a despairing moment I thought our flight into Polynesia's last wilderness might end in frustration. Then, "You go ashore," Ken shouted over the noise of the engine as he taxied close. "I'll watch the clouds." I sighted a plaque erected by an exploration party four years earlier. Cook had been able to anchor so near the shore here in Pickersgill Harbor that trees tangled in the rigging of his *Resolution.*

Scrambling from a float onto a slippery log, I reached shore by crumbling handhold. Birds chimed among the tall trees; I waded through fern in wild wet profusion, and climbed into forest gloom. Man, it seemed, might never have been here.

Yet he had, after all. Here, marvelously surviving among new vegetation, I found stumps of great trees Cook's seamen had felled to make a big clearing for astronomical studies with quadrant and clock that determined New Zealand's precise location. Beside these stumps his crew brewed spruce beer to beat off scurvy, and roasted fresh seal. And here Cook gently charmed the only family of shy Fiordland Maoris to venture near. He found their language recognizably kin to that spoken more than 3,000 miles away on Tahiti.

Now those tribesmen of forest and fiord have gone, mysteriously, with almost no sign to show they have ever been. This is one of the places of Polynesia on which man may never impose, the one place as wild and virgin as when the first human roamer saw it.

Tahiti's warm Matavai Bay already seemed remote in memory, almost beyond recall; I couldn't be farther from palm-girt lagoon. It was difficult to connect one place with the other, yet that was just what the Polynesian voyagers who claimed the South Pacific had done. I had followed their diverse trails across the great ocean of the blue sky. And I had come not only to the limit of their long bright shore; I had come, at last, to the end of their wide, wild world.

Spilling from lofty, mountain-locked Lake Quill (opposite) in Fiordland, icy waters of Sutherland Falls, one of the world's highest, tumble more than 1,900 feet. The middle cascade's massive torrent (left) reduces to toy size a passing helicopter.

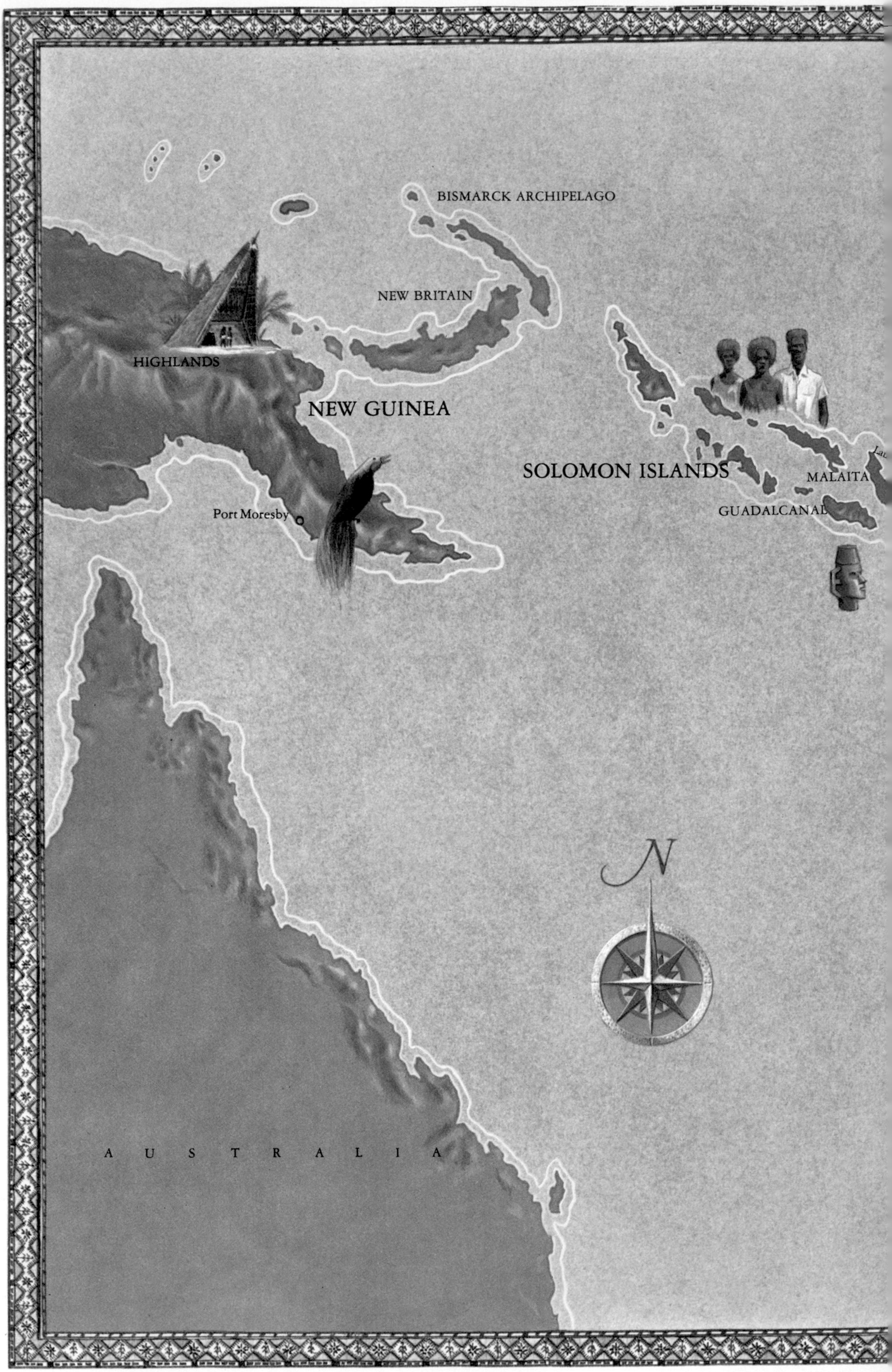

BISMARCK ARCHIPELAGO

NEW BRITAIN

HIGHLANDS

NEW GUINEA

SOLOMON ISLANDS

MALAITA

Port Moresby

GUADALCANAL

N

AUSTRALIA

M E L A N E S I A

Through the "black islands" that lie between the Equator and the Tropic of Capricorn, from Fiji to New Guinea, the dark-skinned people of Melanesia have wrought the most dazzling variety of custom and tradition that any area on earth can display, mile for seagirt mile. Their varied cultures rival their terrain: rain forest on upland slopes, grassland valleys, jungles and coastal swamps and coral islets. In many tongues the Melanesians worked the rites of magic that appease ghosts and shadowy spirits. With red and yellow ocher they brightened masks and ceremonial carvings for the secret world of men gathered in dark clubhouses roofed with thatch. Now new ways and new wealth appear in a region where men traded the currency of gleaming shell and feathers. Australian Olaf Ruhen, author of *Minerva Reef, Land of Dahori,* and other books on the Pacific, reports today's dramatic contrasts of mountain villages, modern factories, cosmopolitan cities.

SANTA CRUZ ISLANDS

NEW HEBRIDES

PENTECOST
ISLAND

Vila

TANNA

LOYALTY ISLANDS

NEW CALEDONIA

Nouméa

FIJI ISLANDS

VANUA LEVU

VITI LEVU
Suva

0   300
STATUTE MILES

Richard Schlecht

CHAPTER SIX

FIJI

Where Polynesia and Melanesia Meet

" WELCOME to our country! We hope you have a happy visit," said a Fijian girl in an ankle-length dress as I arrived at Nandi International Airport. A moment later an Indian woman in a graceful sari greeted me with the same words, and I heard the same proud stress — "*our* country."

I heard that phrase again and again as I traveled through these loved, familiar islands for the first time since the British Crown Colony of Fiji became a fully independent nation on October 10, 1970. And I recognized that a new sense of responsibility seems to have inspired Fiji's mixed population, a new realization that its differing communities — some of them antagonists in the past — can work together for the national good.

On a flight from Nandi to Suva, Fiji's capital and major port, I watched Fijian sailing canoes setting out from mangrove-bordered bays to fish along a tracery of reef. Then fields of sugar cane and pastures of mission grass on the coastal plains gave place to bamboo-tufted hills. For a time we followed a river plumed with rapids and flanked here and there by the thatched huts of Fijian villages.

Mountains slid beneath us, a few foot-tracks tracing steep ridges, until we crossed

In bruising competition, athletes battle over a rugby ball on the island of Viti Levu. Introduced shortly after World War I, the game quickly caught on with the muscular Fijians. Today, they send teams throughout the South Pacific.

JOHN TITCHEN, BLACK STAR

the central divide that separates the dry lee-ward side of Viti Levu from the dense rain forest of the wetter windward side. Almost exactly the size of the Island of Hawaii, rag-gedly beautiful, it supports about 400,000 people. With its neighbor Vanua Levu, next largest of the nation's 300-odd islands, it con-tains 87 percent of the land and more than nine-tenths of Fiji's 534,811 people.

Of these, only 230,480 are Fijian by des-cent. Indians outnumber them: 271,031 who throng the cities and agricultural areas of the main islands. Nearly all are descended from indentured laborers imported three or four generations back to work on the sugar plan-tations—Fijians of the time had little interest in working for someone else.

The Indians—Hindus, Sikhs, or Moslems

—have kept many of their religious beliefs and customs. Some have prospered as towns-folk, in trade or professions. Most remain farmers, on leased land.

Tongans, Rotumans, Samoans, Solomon Islanders, Gilbertese, Chinese, Europeans, and others have made Fiji their home.

This mixture, and especially the Indians' numerical majority, has led to much concern over racial problems. Though these exist, and will continue to arise, the country's leaders do not consider them insoluble.

"What you have to remember is that Fijian society has traditionally been an amalgam—of Polynesian and Melanesian and then of European influence," says Ratu Sir Kamisese Mara, K.B.E., the new nation's first Prime Minister. A commanding representative of

118

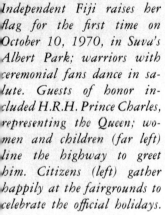

Independent Fiji raises her flag for the first time on October 10, 1970, in Suva's Albert Park; warriors with ceremonial fans dance in salute. Guests of honor included H.R.H. Prince Charles, representing the Queen; women and children (far left) line the highway to greet him. Citizens (left) gather happily at the fairgrounds to celebrate the official holidays.

the high chiefs who formerly ruled Fiji, well-muscled and lithe, he stands 6 feet 4 inches tall; and his own titles illustrate the richness of Fiji's varied heritage.

Ratu in Fijian approximates "lord." "Sir" reveals his English knighthood. "Kamisese" recalls an honor bestowed on an ancestor by one of the great high chiefs of Samoa. Headline writers often refer to him as the "Tui Lau," "king" or leader of the Lau group. These, Fiji's easternmost islands, mark the farthest penetration of Melanesians into the South Pacific, and their contacts or conflicts with Polynesians from Tonga. Here the first Wesleyan missionaries in Fiji began their work—most Fijians today are Christians.

"Under the British Empire," explains Sir Kamisese, "the role of the Indians was first

seen as a temporary one; indeed, this was taken for granted until the 1920's. When it was clear that the Indians would stay, the policy of 'Fiji for the Fijians' had long been established, at least by the land laws."

These laws generally reserved ownership of land to Fijians, and prevented Indians from buying properties they farmed.

"The Indians grew determined to fight for a place in the Fijian sun. Our first constitutional conference in 1965 recognized that they had a part to play, and the 1970 constitution for independence laid down clearly that everyone born in Fiji has equal rights. Thus we reached independence with all the people in a participating mood."

Ratu Mara—as friends still call him—led me to an ultramodern operations room as he

119

outlined the problems Fiji faces in economic development. In 1969 imports totaling $77,-888,146 (in Fijian dollars) overshadowed $53,226,146 in exports. Rapidly increasing tourism promised help—"Copra has to be freighted," said the Prime Minister with a smile; "tourists freight themselves." He outlined new methods of agriculture, an intensive geological survey, studies of deep-sea fishing methods, and other projects, adding, "We look to the future with some confidence, especially considering our strategic position as the hub of transport in the Pacific."

He cited other factors that promise Fiji a leading role: the Pacific Producers Association, a group of countries with related economic interests; the Fiji School of Medicine, the University of the South Pacific, and the Pacific Theological College. I commented on the growing cooperation among Christians in the Pacific, and he smiled: "Perhaps our islands' distance and small size makes us think that God is not solely concerned with the sect to which we might belong." Reflectively, he added: "One thing I particularly admire in the Hindu religion is the strength of family

TED SPIEGEL, RAPHO GUILLUMETTE (BELOW), JACK FIELDS (UPPER RIGHT), AND MICHAEL E. LONG, NATIONAL GEOGRAPHIC STAFF

life. Our problems with juveniles are smallest in the Indian community."

Humor, athletics, and a proud past are strong bonds. In the elevators of the new government office block, the imposing stature of many Fijian administrators makes total weight the only reliable guide to capacity, so the figure showing the number of riders permitted has been obliterated. The offices themselves overlook Albert Park, a sports ground where wildly enthusiastic teams—Fijian and Indian—play rugby, soccer, or cricket. Here, at the Annual Meeting

Deepwater harbor of Suva holds cargo and cruise ships; on a downtown street an open-air bus awaits a policeman's signal. Shoppers in Nandi include Indians in flowing saris. Indians first came to Fiji in 1879 as plantation laborers. Today, they number more than half the islands' 534,811 people. 121

Nail-polish beauty spots highlight the face of a young Indian girl preparing for her wedding. She wears a silk sari woven with glittering thread.

JACK FIELDS

Masked by a headdress of tinsel, flowers, and mirrors, a Hindu bridegroom (above) stands before a brass bowl of incense held by his future mother-in-law. He traditionally hides his face from the bride until the ceremony. After exchanging vows, the garlanded couple (left) sits before an altar decked with blossoms, and hears the chants of a priest exhorting them to remain faithful.

of Co-operative Societies, villagers may perform *mekes* — renderings of song and dance — from morning to night.

Nearby lie the Public Gardens, where every tropical flower seems to thrive, from cannas in circus-wagon hues to misty-blue plumbagos. Here a museum offers spectacular evidence of Fiji's past maritime glories — such as a canoe's steering oar that took seven men to handle. Farther on, at the gates of Government House, a sentry in belted red tunic and spotless white *sulu,* or kilt, keeps ceremonial guard for the representative of Elizabeth II, Queen of Fiji.

Across the road from Albert Park stands the Grand Pacific Hotel, built in 1914 and a Suva institution. To seaward, when tides and seasons are right, Fijian matrons stand waist-deep in the harbor, netting fish.

In the business center a crowd jostles past shops and offices: tiny Indian women with nose jewels, tall, muscular Fijians, Australians and New Zealanders in shorts and socks. Visitors throng the streets when cruise ships disgorge as many as 1,600 passengers each for a day of shopping — many goods are duty-free. Tourists buy not only appliances and luxury items, but also local carved wood and patterned baskets, brooches and bracelets of tortoise-shell and mother-of-pearl.

Beyond the shops the Municipal Market sprawls beside the piers. Fijian women with chocolate skins and mop hairdos mingle with wavy-haired Polynesians from Tonga, Rotuma, and Samoa. They load themselves with yams, taro roots, cassava, tomatoes, greens. On the vegetables in their capacious baskets they stow fish, clams, a string of crabs, or *kai,* freshwater mussels for which smiling women comb the river currents.

At the piers, trading schooners from the outer islands supply the markets and deliver copra to exporters. I boarded *Maroro,* one of these schooners, to visit the northern Lau group — where, in the days of pagan wars, ran the frontier between Melanesian and Polynesian. Here, throughout periods of uneasy peace, Tongans traded with Fijians for earthenware pots, for sandalwood, for clubs, spears, and wooden bowls, and canoes sometimes more than 100 feet in length.

Fijian fire walkers on Mbengga Island emerge without so much as a blister after striding across a pit filled with searingly hot stones. Damp leaves spread during the ceremony raise clouds of vapor. Assistants (opposite) prepare the pit by raking aside embers of logs used to heat the rocks. Skeptical observers come away convinced that they have seen no trickery. Indians follow a similar custom, walking on embers instead of stones.

My destination was Naitaumba, one of the few freehold islands in the archipelago. It now belongs in part to actor Raymond Burr. But Naitaumba is no simple retreat from an actor's public life. Two-thirds of the 3,000-acre island is under coconuts; its 175 people work on the plantation.

With his partner, Burr has planted stands of teak, mahogany, and macadamia trees; started a garden of orchids; stocked cattle in a modern dairy; set cover plantings of new grasses like the Koronivia developed by a Fijian government research station; improved housing for his workmen; and begun a program to increase production.

Such widening of economic activity, with a greater range of jobs, may check the drift of people—especially the young—to the two main islands from a hundred others. Tourism, for example, is only now beginning to spread to a few smaller islands.

I found a new hotel, one of the South Pacific's extensive TraveLodge chain, preparing for opening day on Taveuni, known as the Garden of Fiji for the wealth of its flora. A ten-mile-long range of volcanic cones dominates its 168 square miles. Fiji's European discoverer, Abel Tasman, sighted these peaks on the night of February 5, 1643.

Rain drenches the cliffs of the east coast as they catch the southeast trades, and spectacular waterfalls cascade into the sea. Inland,

125

great chasms intersect the mountains. Most residents believe them to shelter a half-monster, half-man who can smash down the tough lantana undergrowth in his progress, leaving tracks that look like they were made by enormous human feet.

Fijians attribute such tracks to the *Veli*, a traditional spirit of mountain and rain forest who teaches new songs to the songmakers when they approach him with a due and solitary reverence — as a visitor should.

Shaded from the scorching sun, an Indian woman and her daughter wait beside hilly Queens Road for a bus to Nandi, some 15 miles away. Below, volcanic peaks rise from rolling plains that nurture fields of sugar cane, Fiji's major export crop.

MICHAEL E. LONG, NATIONAL GEOGRAPHIC STAFF

Across Somosomo Strait, at Savusavu on Vanua Levu, drifts of steam haunt a palm-fringed beach where small boiling springs burst out among fragmented coral. The Hot Springs Hotel looks down on an arm of the sea where sailing canoes ferry produce to market, and the road always seems to hold a procession of gossiping villagers.

Flying back to Suva, I looked down on the strait William Bligh sailed during his epic 3,600-mile journey after the *Bounty* mutineers set him and 18 others adrift in a 23-foot boat near Tonga. Just beyond the strait, now called Bligh Water, two Fijian sailing canoes bore swiftly down on him.

Bligh took no chances. A few days earlier he had touched at Tofua, in western Tonga, and islanders had killed one of his crew. With fear to drive them, his men bent to the oars, escaping into the open sea. Bligh eventually reached Timor, completing the most celebrated open-boat voyage of all time.

In far more agreeable circumstances, on a previous visit to Fiji, I enjoyed an open-boat trip inland — up the Wainimila, a major tributary of the Rewa, Fiji's biggest river. I traveled with Vula Saumaiwai, the *Roko Tui* — then the chief administrator of Naitasiri Province. Among Fijians Vula settled land disputes, acted as a village adviser, and officiated in tax collection and financial matters.

I met Vula at Serea, a hill village far up the river, and we boarded a "putt-putt," a flat-bottomed outboard 35 feet long and less than 4 feet wide. Vula took the tiller, and we set out. Cattle waded in shallow backwaters, and distant mountains quivered pale blue in the heat against a cobalt sky.

The river formed the only highway here, and we passed bamboo rafts laden with taro and bananas for the Suva market. At no time were we alone, for the riversides danced with shrieking children splashing in the shallows.

A bend in the river brought us suddenly to a village called Nairukuruku. Laughing men and women were throwing each other into the current, or drenching the unsuspecting with buckets of water. Though it was January 10, they were still celebrating the New Year. They were also building a new Methodist church. Every now and then a man or woman

Keeping alive a centuries-old rite of their forebears in India, Hindu fire walkers move in ceremonious procession to a pit of smoldering embers near the town of Nausori. A practitioner of the ritual carries a pan to collect offerings of coins from bystanders along the route. An old woman, her nose pierced with gold jewelry, preserves another of her people's customs. Silver trident of the Hindu god Siva skewers the face of one of the fire walkers; ashes smudge neck, cheek, and forehead.

would abandon skylarking to carry a building stone or bucket of gravel for concrete some 200 yards to the construction site.

"This is a way we have in Fiji," the Roko Tui said. "If we have heavy community work, such as repairing trails, we sometimes take it in the form of play. Thus the work grows

JACK FIELDS (ABOVE) AND MICHAEL E. LONG, NATIONAL GEOGRAPHIC STAFF

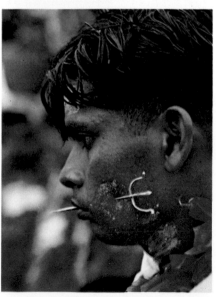

light." Four years later, such holiday efforts had virtually completed the church.

Preparations for a Fijian kava ceremony of welcome usually proceed without flurry, as Vula and I found at Nairukuruku. Women had spread new mats on the floor of a large house and set out a hand-carved wooden bowl almost three feet across. They were still standing at their work when we entered and sat down. As they finished each small task they clapped their hands softly in apology because their heads were higher than ours.

"It is *tambu* to stand or to reach for anything above a superior who is sitting," the Roko Tui explained.

White cowrie shells decorated a long coconut fiber cord attached to the bowl and stretched toward us, the guests of honor. Some 70 men drifted in and sat cross-legged in their allotted places on the floor. The kava maker, seated on a log, grated green root of the pepper plant with a knife, then vigorously worked the pulp into a ball. As an assistant added water, the kava maker kneaded the pulp to extract the juices.

A master of ceremonies watched carefully. When the drink reached just the right consistency, he cried, *"Lomba"* — "Squeeze." The kava maker swirled a strainer of shredded hibiscus bark through the grayish-brown liquid. Then he clapped his hands sharply three times. The master of ceremonies promptly ordered, *"Talo"* — "Pour it out."

The cupbearer, dressed in a cotton sulu decorated at the belt with green leaves, approached and presented the *mbilo,* a coconut shell cut in half and highly polished. On the tips of his toes, he lowered himself with knees bent, bare back ramrod straight, arms outstretched, hands clasping the cup.

The brewer filled the mbilo, and the bearer raised himself to full height. To chants and handclapping, veins bulging with the strain of the exacting ritual, he carried the cup to the Roko Tui. After Vula drained it, he tossed

Spoon-shaped bracts of the Medinilla spectabilis *hang in clusters on Taveuni, a volcanic island called the Garden of Fiji because of its rich, deep soil. A newly discovered species known only on Taveuni, spectabilis got its name in 1967.*

it spinning like a top onto the mat. Then all present cried *"A matha"* in a deep, gutteral tone: *"A matha"* — "It is dry."

Some observers have said that kava is intoxicating; some, that it affects the gait. Certainly I have sometimes felt a muscular weakness after hours of sitting with crossed legs, but the only effect I can truly ascribe to kava is that of cooling and refreshing.

Continuing upriver, we called at other mountain villages: Saumakia, Navuniyasi, Nawala, Korosuli. All are shrinking as young people seek an education or answer the lure of the city, leaving the pleasures of home.

We coasted downriver in rain so dense we could hardly see the rapids, while people swam and shouted in the storm. Some fished with nets along the major reaches. It seemed incredible that a century ago Fijians fortified their villages for safety from tribal wars.

Thoughts of those combats colored my recent flight over the eastern coast of Viti Levu and the shore-flanking island of Mbau. I marveled at the power this 20-acre isle once exerted. At its height it harbored more than 3,000 people and a hundred war canoes. Twenty temples occupied the central plain, their lofty rooftrees topping a steep thatch. Houses crowded the land elsewhere, so close that any fire threatened all.

After unscrupulous sailors and traders introduced firearms in the early 19th century, Fijian chiefs gained greater power. In the 1850's the High Chief Thakombau — "the Destroyer of Mbau" — used muskets and cannon to subdue most of western Fiji.

Cannibalism, already notorious, had increased. After the battle of Verata on Viti Levu in 1839, Thakombau and his father Tanoa gave 260 bodies of men, women, and children to friends and allied chiefs.

I visited Mbau once on a day of pouring rain, and as I drank kava in the provincial offices I looked out over a green that must cover a tangle of splintered human bones. Children play rugby there now, and nearby stands Fiji's first Christian church, soundly built with stone walls three feet thick.

The baptismal font within is a large, white-painted stone. Thakombau knew it as his

Descendants of warriors, Fijians brandish spears in a vigorous ceremonial war dance performed for feasts and other special occasions. The men paint their faces with charcoal and wear frangipani leis and skirts of shredded leaves. Musicians sit cross-legged, chanting to keep time as they drum the ground with lengths of bamboo.

skull crusher. A thousand people, swung against it by executioners, spilled their lives upon it. But just 15 years after the carnage of Verata, Thakombau became a Christian and prohibited cannibalism on Mbau. In 1867 he became a king, crowned by European residents seeking a stable government in Fiji to protect their trading interests.

I visited his grave on a nearby hill, and recognized the ragged tree beside it as sandalwood, the tree that first brought the European to Fiji. High prices in China had long made sandalwood the world's most valuable tree. Early in the 19th century, ship after ship stopped in Fiji to load the fragrant wood, and some captains offered their ships and crews in tribal wars, paying for their cargoes with the lives of human beings.

Making kava, *a traditional Pacific island beverage, a Fijian squeezes a mixture of cold water and the grated root of a pepper plant through a strainer of hibiscus-bark fiber. Fijians serve the drink both informally and in an intricate ceremony that forms the nucleus of island social life.*

Commerce once promised new life for the island of Ovalau, where my aircraft landed. The town of Levuka clings sleepily to the base of steep hills on the east, bordering a little-used harbor. In the 1850's residents expected that a proposed Panama canal would foster shipping, and they could offer a port of call on the sea lanes to Australia and New Zealand. Their town did become a capital on October 10, 1874. Then, by Deed of Cession, Thakombau conveyed his realm to his "Lady Queen," Victoria. But trade passed to Suva, and in 1882 government followed.

I returned myself, tantalized by the variety still awaiting me. I would have liked to go back to Vatukoula, where a modern mine makes gold Fiji's third largest export, ranked after sugar and coconut products. I would gladly have sailed east to the craggy island of Koro, a shark's tooth of volcanic rock where men possess the strange power of summoning giant turtles from the sea.

From my Suva hotel I could see Mbengga Island, mysterious because of the unexplained ability of some of its thousand inhabitants to walk barefoot across searingly hot stones. If the rite loses something of awe when performed on schedule at hotels on Viti Levu, as it is today, the mystery remains.

133

I would always welcome a chance to return
to the Yasawa Group, a ribbon of beach-girt
coral islands stretching northward along the
horizon west of Viti Levu. Once, with a dozen
other guests on a local cruise vessel, I enjoyed the hospitality of bays and reefs and
markets. On Nambukeru, after dark in a lan-
tern-lighted hall, a well-drilled chorus of girls
and men entertained us with resonant har-
monies — dancing to spirited battle chants or
plaintive love songs. To cotton garments in

*Jalopy-borne clowns parade in Nandi during the
Bula Festival, a week-long revel held each July.
Bright strips of crepe paper, daubs of charcoal,
and a scrap of plastic make a costume for one
youngster. Jumper-clad girls and a Fiji Military
Forces band march briskly in the tropical sun.*

JACK FIELDS (ABOVE) AND MICHAEL E. LONG, NATIONAL GEOGRAPHIC STAFF

prints of red and gold and green, they added skirts of dyed shredded fiber and ornaments of leaves: armlets, wreaths, and crowns. All too soon their conductor, with gestures of perfect precision and dignity, led the strains of "Isa Lei," Fiji's haunting song of farewell.

The highlight of the cruise was swimming in the caves of Sawa-i-Lau, an elevated limestone island. Its sheer gray ramparts, covered with light scrub, give no indication of the vaulted tunnels within. But an easy climb brought us to the entrance, and we clambered down massive boulders to a dimly lighted freshwater pool. Its still depths strike cool after the sun-warmed currents of the Yasawa lagoons. Floating in the shadowy grotto, visitors gaze up towering stone walls to the broken ceiling, where green leaves flicker in the distant sunshine, and murmur with awe, "It's like swimming in a cathedral!"

Underwater tunnels lead into an unlighted cavern, an eerie place many visitors avoid. They prefer to watch Fijian crewmen climb the limestone, crevice by crevice, to high natural platforms and leap or dive skillfully into the main pool. Their rollicking humor dispels the uncanny mood, and the party ends with shouts of laughter. But now I wanted to sample things that promise Fiji new importance in the world's largest ocean.

One, of course, is the carrier Air Pacific, originally Fiji Airways. Its flights now link New Guinea, the Solomons, the New Hebrides, the Gilberts, Nauru, Samoa, and Tonga, with Nandi and other Fijian centers.

Yet the linking of minds may prove most important of all. On a sunny morning when the view seemed as limitless as the Pacific itself, I drove out from Suva to the Fiji School of Medicine, formerly the Central Medical School, remembering a remark of Ratu Mara's: "In my studies of medicine as a young man, I found that disease does not choose races."

I passed a model village where a cooperative preserves Fiji's past for interested visitors, and at the hilltop beyond paused to admire the school's location.

In 1971 the school had 119 students, 24 of them women. "Every major group in the Pa-

cific has been sending women with the exception of Tonga," the Principal, Dr. Guy Hawley, told me. "We get students from all over the Pacific—twice we even had them from British Honduras—and train them in either medicine or dentistry."

Since 1968 the University of the South Pacific has taken over the first-year premedical courses and those designed to bridge the gap between college-level undergraduate requirements and the varying attainments of island educational systems. It opened with 160 students from 11 major island groups, with the King of Tonga as chancellor. I found an old friend from Tonga as its Resources and External Relations Officer, Inoke Faletau, and he guided me over the 192-acre campus, splendidly located beyond the quiet hilltop suburbs northeast of Suva, at Lauthala Bay.

Here the Royal New Zealand Air Force had maintained a flying-boat base.

"The New Zealand government made us a present of it, with about 200 buildings of various sizes, so we were able to begin operations immediately," Inoke explained. "In spite of that, we still need buildings for residences and permanent lecture rooms. Now we have a full-time enrollment of 640—with part-time students, close to 800.

"One of the things we've started, with United Nations assistance, is a curriculum development unit to cope with the diversity of educational systems in the Pacific."

Near the sea, the steep hills of the campus level out. Some of the flying-boat hangars are devoted to biological laboratories; others shelter the boats of a university sailing club. All around us, among the flowers and the lush tropical greenery, were groups of students, astonishingly varied in race and origins.

"It's an exciting campus," Inoke smiled. "So much to be done, and so many people finding the best way to do it."

And his words, I concluded, summed up my impressions of the nation of Fiji.

Honeymooners roam a palm-fringed beach below volcanic cliffs on Waya Island in the Yasawa Group off Viti Levu. Lured by sand and sun, increasing thousands of Pacific travelers visit Fiji, a crossroad for international jets and ships.

CHAPTER SEVEN

NEW CALEDONIA

An Echo of France in a Mineral-rich Land

BEYOND THE AIRCRAFT WINDOW, New Caledonia thrust jaggedly from the sea, row on row of high, mineral-rich mountains, many of them scarred red by open-cut mines. Looking down, I watched ocean rollers break into pluming surf against the island's barrier reef, an almost unbroken line of white five or six miles off the coast. Between reef and shore the bright blue waters of the lagoon sparkled in the sun.

Except for the mines, the island appeared almost as Captain Cook had seen it when he approached from the north in September, 1774. "Indeed if it was not for the Fertility of the Planes and some few spotts in the Mountains," he wrote, "the Country would be called a D[r]eary waste, the Mountains and other high places are for the Most part incapable of Cultivation, consisting chiefly of solid Rocks...."

The white ribbon of surf and coral reef, the blue of the lagoon, and the swatches of red on the mountains seemed especially fitting colors for New Caledonia, for they echo those of the French *tricolore* that flies over this island Territory. And the whole basks in an ideally balanced climate with temperatures ranging from an average of 66° F. in

Molten ferro-nickel streams into molds at a smelter on New Caledonia. Led only by Canada and the Soviet Union as a nickel producer, the island annually yields more than 65,000 tons of the metal, exported mainly to France and Japan.

JACK FIEL

winter to 78° in the hot season of December through March.

New Caledonia, halfway between Fiji and Australia, is a baton-shaped island 240 miles long and 30 in average breadth, and covering 6,230 square miles. I thought it even larger as I sat hypnotized by the procession of craggy mountains. A meandering tracery of roads connected the gashes of the mines.

Though the island lies on the same line of volcanic upheaval as the New Hebrides to the north and New Zealand to the south, geologists have found little volcanic ash or lava, only ore-laden mountains. The metamorphic rocks hold copper, gold, silver, and lead; the serpentine rocks yield chrome, cobalt, iron—and nickel.

New Caledonia ranks third, after Canada and the Soviet Union, in the world production of nickel. Its ores, exploited for more than 50 years, support a newly expanding industry for Space Age technology.

The pilot avoided the highest of the ranges by crossing the island near the southern tip, and soon I looked down on Nouméa, the capital and, with approximately 45,000 people, the largest town.

I had arranged to meet my wife Madeleine here, and we stayed at the luxury Nouméa Hotel on the Baie des Citrons. Five other major tourist hotels stand on a beach-bordered peninsula outside the harbor.

Our first morning on the island Madeleine noticed an outrigger canoe hauled up on the beach. "Do you think we could possibly hire it?" she asked, and the desk clerk smiled.

"It's yours," he said. "Use it whenever you like. Just return the paddles when you finish."

We spent hours each day looking through crystal water at coral, visiting the islands that guard the bay, watching spearfishermen glide into the depths like goggle-eyed Neptunes.

Under the spell of sea and sun, we had to persuade ourselves to leave the water. Then we would catch one of a stream of tiny blue buses to the Place des Cocotiers, four blocks of lawns and gardens where the coconut palms that give this city square its name rear tufted heads above the red and orange blossoms of the poinciana trees.

Here at the top of a gentle slope stands the large St. Joseph de Cluny convent school. Three times a day, morning, evening, and throughout the long lunch period, hordes of young girls race and skip among flowerbeds already gay with marigolds and canna lilies. On yellow wooden benches and around the rim of the fountain they sit—Asians, Pacific islanders, and Europeans, all dressed alike in demure gray skirts and crisp white blouses.

About four in the afternoon, small boys with adult-size satchels start home from their own classes. Some munch *petit pains,* crusty miniature loaves; some stop to shoot marbles on the paved walks. They exchange terse remarks—*"Allez allez!"* "okee-doke!"—while the girls chatter like starlings.

"Prenez garde!" one shouted, and I swung

"Paris of the Pacific," capital of the French Overseas Territory of New Caledonia, Nouméa prospers as a maritime center. A veil of smoke rises from the nickel smelter on Pointe Doniambo, beyond the urban center. Coves and bays give the city a long and lovely shoreline; pleasure craft cluster at moorings of the Yacht Club in the Baie des Pêcheurs, where boats arrive frequently from Fiji, New Zealand, and Australia. A Navy building stands on the point in the foreground. With new firms entering the island's nickel industry, new personnel arriving, Nouméa grows richer, busier, and more crowded. In a downtown boutique, fashion-conscious girls study a new design from La France Métropole, *half a world away.*

around to find that Madeleine had stepped into traffic, forgetting that New Caledonians drive on the right, not on the left as Australians do. A Frenchman in a beret helped her back to the curb.

"More like Paris every day," he said in English with only a trace of accent.

But the "Paris of the Pacific" has taken on a touch of boomtown since the demand and prices for nickel rose sharply in 1970. Of course, most Nouméans are French. On mainland New Caledonia less than half the people are Melanesians, and most of these live away from the city. The population includes a few Arabs and Somalis and West Indians; Asians; Polynesians from Wallis Island.

Now a labor shortage draws workers from islands near and far. Tahitians who learned their skills at nuclear test sites find construction jobs easily. A thousand Indonesians have helped on building projects. An unskilled man who can earn $2.50 a day in the New Hebrides can earn $6.50 on New Caledonia, and return home with money saved.

Nickel executives and engineers have taken hotel rooms for months, but tourists come as well — 14,386 in 1970. Australians and New Zealanders enjoy the Continental flavor of an island a few hours from home by jet.

Madeleine made herself at home in Nouméa, shopping for French perfume and fashions. She took her time, wandering from shop to shop one morning, and she sounded aggrieved when the first door closed on her.

"It's only eleven o'clock!" she complained. But the key had turned, and when we looked

MICHAEL E. LONG, NATIONAL GEOGRAPHIC STAFF (TWO CENTER PICTURES), AND JACK FIELDS

Diversity and joie de vivre *stamp the faces of New Caledonia: Melanesian stockman, cowhide whip over his shoulder, pauses during work on a 7,000-acre cattle station. Octogenarian F. J. P. Martin (now deceased) was descended from a 19th-century English seaman, one of the first settlers from Europe. Lofting a metal ball, a Nouméan plays* pétanque, *a game somewhat like lawn bowling. In a blur of speed a cyclist races in Olympic Stadium at Magenta, a suburb of Nouméa. A teaching nun on the Isle of Pines reflects the quiet confidence of her faith, and a Melanesian youth, with a hibiscus behind his ear, epitomizes unhurried life in New Caledonia. A girl of five wears delicate rings in her pierced ears. A water skier slaloms off Nouméa; a cricketer swings vigorously at a ball.*

around, we saw that all the other shops had followed suit.

New Caledonians take a three-hour lunch break, and they eat well. The hotel dining rooms seem to achieve near-perfection. We also found memorable eating adventure in small cafes. Families operate restaurants like Le Coq d'Or, or La Potinière.

"You are enjoying my little specialty?" beams the moustached proprietor over *coq au vin,* tender chicken in a delicate wine sauce, or *champignons provençale,* mushrooms seasoned with garlic and parsley, or a fluffy golden omelette flavored with tangy cheese. And he asks the question with a certain confidence, for he has neglected nothing in preparation and serving. He caters to every taste except that of the man in a hurry.

In one of the city's pleasant residential areas, Georges and Simone Dreux entertained us at their home. Simone, born in New Caledonia, is mother of two husky boys and — at intervals — warden of Dalmatian puppies. Her husband, employed by *Société Le Nickel,* was one of the many younger Frenchmen who came here after World War II.

"Europe is too constricting," he said, "too many pressures, and there aren't many other places left where a Frenchman can go to make his fortune and live in a French way in a French community." He laughed. "Well, no fortune, but where can I find a better life? All the weekends on the boat, fishing; the beautiful sea and the sunshine; the wonderful climate." In glass-fronted cabinets he displayed a collection of seashells that would have been the envy of a conchologist.

Sea creatures enticed us to the Nouméa Aquarium, founded in 1956 by Dr. René Catala and his wife Stucki. With patient expertise they have succeeded in displaying living creatures of the reefs in natural groupings: coral, cuttlefish, wrasses, pearly nautilus, sea snakes. Overhearing a visitor asking what the specimens are made of, he says: "All are alive, *Madame* — even me!" Discovering that rare deepwater corals glow with color under ultraviolet light, he has devised darkened tanks to show them off. Madeleine and I found startling patterns and colors: orange with crevices of smoky amethyst; a scintillating blue, flecked with buttercup yellow; a jolting lime green.

But Dr. Catala notes sadly that a denser population with its detergents and wastes threatens the beauty he knows so well. "Ten years ago I could cross the road, go 40 paces into the water, and find myself in the undisturbed splendor of a fringing reef. Now it looks like the moon — all dead. And many other reef islands have met the same fate."

Averting just such problems of pollution is one concern of the South Pacific Commission, established in 1947 by the six governments then administering island groups — France, Australia, the Netherlands, New Zealand, Britain, and the United States. From its beach-front headquarters in Nouméa,

Springing from a coral ledge, a spearfisherman takes flying aim at his quarry off Mouly Island near New Caledonia. After a successful leap, a grinning islander clambers back, his catch impaled on a pronged spear. At left, a sea hunter subdues an East Pacific green turtle. To capture the creature, a popular island food, he waits for it to nap on the surface, then flips it helpless onto its back.

JACK FIELDS

Sea slug's flowerlike egg mass
(1) clings to a rock in the Nouméa
Aquarium, a marine research
center founded in 1956 by biol-
ogist René Catala and his wife,
Mme Catala-Stucki. In 1957 the
couple discovered that certain
deepwater corals glow with
luminescent colors when sub-
mitted to ultraviolet light. Devis-
ing displays in darkened tanks,
the Catalas gathered performers
for their science show from the
barrier reef that encircles New
Caledonia. Lobed coral (2), wearing a mantle of flesh over a stony
skeleton, resembles molten lava
when under ultraviolet rays. Fragile, fanlike shelf coral (3) takes
its color from microscopic
Zooxanthellae algae within its
polyps; mushroom coral attaches
at the base. Scarlet *Favites* (4) a
dull beige in ordinary light, glows
red on a base of green shelf
coral. Tentacles of an alcyonarian
(5) undulate with the movement
of the water. Colonies of con-
voluted coral (6) help build reefs
throughout the South Pacific.

1

4

5

6

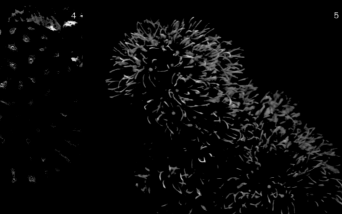

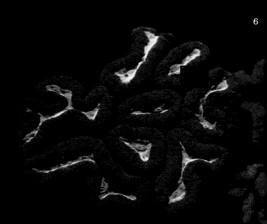

it provides research and technical assistance on health, social, and economic problems.

"We concentrate on advisory services," reported Acting Secretary-General John E. deYoung in 1971, "and we want qualified islanders for staff as rapidly as possible. We train the trainers. At our community education center in Suva, our expert from the University of Minnesota is in her last year; an islander from the counterpart staff will take her place. They work out teaching methods — how to teach women accustomed to cooking on three stones various new ways, including the uses of an electric range."

Often islanders want aid in teaching English as a second language, and the Commission publishes readers carefully prepared to interest children of the Pacific — with stories of village elders and witches, breadfruit and mango trees, canoe trips and new tricycles, a New Guinea boy adopted by a crocodile, and Cinderella. Coloring books explain that a cup goes with a saucer.

"The great potential in the islands," says Mr. deYoung, "is young people."

Member nations are changing. The Netherlands withdrew when it lost its holding in New Guinea; Western Samoa joined after its separation from New Zealand in 1962. Tonga has not become a member; but the 5,263-acre Republic of Nauru, independent since 1968, has, and so has Fiji.

In its varied programs, the SPC has help from the U.N. and from national agencies such as the French overseas scientific and technical research organization, ORSTOM. At Nouméa, ORSTOM anthropologists analyze the change from the islands' old, balanced subsistence economy to cash — and point out the social risks involved.

With data from the entire southwest Pacific, geophysicists study the changing relationships between oceans and continents.

Entomologists seek natural parasites or predators to control the rhinoceros beetle, an insect almost the size of a cigarette pack, which kills coconut palms by boring into the budding fronds; the cane pest *Lepidosaphos beckii;* a fruit-sucking moth. "Islands are natural labs for such work," says one; "so we can limit DDT, you know.

"Here our rivers are not carrying pesticides yet, but mining effluents — you see from the air the red patches at the mouths of rivers, *hélas.*"

Any problem or benefit from nickel mining can be expected to increase. Société Le Nickel, which dominated the New Caledonia industry for years, has new rivals from Canada, the U. S., and Japan as well as France. Development planned for the next decade may cost more than a billion dollars, if projected mines and smelters and supporting towns become reality throughout the island.

And in that case I shall be all the happier to have seen its countryside and villages as Madeleine and I found them. We were still in the rainy season, which from December through March can immobilize much country traffic. Between floods Madeleine and I set out in a hired car to see the island. The vegetation, much of it unique to New Caledonia, was all new and strange to her. We drove through a savanna of *niaoulis,* slender trees with dull white bark and delicate pale leaves, that rose ghostlike on either side of us.

Then Madeleine recognized the lantana

Open-cut mine of the French-owned Société Le Nickel *scars mountain ridges high above New Caledonia's east coast. Helmeted miners extract the ore with huge power shovels for transport by truck and by rail to the Nouméa smelter. The island's mountains also hold deposits of chrome, iron, manganese, copper, cobalt, and tungsten.*

JACK FIELDS

bush that spread over the hills once terraced by native gardeners. But ...

"What are those yellow globes?" she asked.

I stopped the car and brought her back a dozen of the yellow guavas, pink-fleshed and ripe, that hung everywhere in a tangle of what seemed a waste of scrub. She had already eaten the cooked fruit; guava jam is a standby of every New Caledonian family.

At Bouloupari, 53 miles north of Nouméa on the west-coast road, we lunched on enormous slabs of ham and crusty French rolls washed down with a rough claret. Outside, a flightless bird, the size of a small rooster and beautiful in soft-gray plumage, stepped up and down in a small yard, stretching wings striped black, brown, and white.

"It is a *cagou*, our 'national' bird," the innkeeper explained. "And it is unique to this country, very rare, with little chance of living free, for the dogs can catch it. It can't run fast enough to escape them."

Some village hotels keep one or two in captivity, a practice that could mean a reprieve for the bird, already on the edge of extinction.

The island's animals and plants fascinated me, and later I spoke about the flora with Mr. Lawrie Johnson, a botanist of the National Herbarium in Sydney.

"New Caledonia has an extremely rich flora for its size, about 3,000 species," he explained. "Of these, some are found in neighboring countries—Australia or New Zealand, or on the islands to the north—but about three-quarters are confined to this one island. So you see why biologists regard New Caledonia as one of the most interesting islands in the world."

On that point Madeleine and I found ourselves in complete agreement with the biologists. After staying the night at Bourail, the island's second-largest town, we followed a winding road through precipitous passes to the east coast. From a mountain gap, the Col des Roussettes, named for the large red-

furred fruit bats of the region, we gazed down on the Houaïlou Valley, rich, peaceful, beautiful. Farther on, missions, churches, wayside crosses alternated with blue patches of sea dotted with fishing canoes. We caught a glimpse of a fisherman, spear poised above the shallow waters of the reef.

We looked in on villages of the Ny and Pothé tribes. At each, a sign carried the names of the village and its chief. The houses, some traditionally round with conical roofs but some rectangular, stood in tidy, flower-decked grounds. A woman at a fire roasted coffee beans on a sheet of iron, and called to

Under easy sail, an outrigger glides in shallows among scrub-topped islets in the Baie d'Oupi on the east coast of the Isle of Pines, a dependency of New Caledonia. Visitors as well as islanders find excellent fishing within the fringing reefs.

friends hilling sweet potatoes nearby. Most of them wore bright Mother Hubbards.

In Cook's time the women dressed in "a short Petticoat made of the small filaments of the Plantain." He described the inhabitants as "a strong robust active well made people, Courteous and friendly and not in the least addicted to pelfering," and their circular houses as "something like Behives and full as close and warm. The side walls are about 4½ feet high, but the roof is high and peaked to a point above which is a post...."

Cook might have added that the posts, or roof spires, resemble totem poles, frequently bearing fearsome faces—stylized representations of ancestors. Except that the walls of the houses are higher and the people dressed in cloth, his descriptions are valid today.

As we moved up the east coast, we had to wait for punts to ferry us across each of the larger rivers, the Tchamba, Tiwaka, and Tipindjé. A heavy cable stretching across the river ran through pulleys on one side of the craft, keeping it on course. Madeleine at first exclaimed in surprise as a lithe boatman leaped to the taut cable, grasped an upright beam, and pushed the punt as he trudged along. "Surely he's not going to push all this

Towering short-branched pines astounded sailors who likened them to pillars of stone when Cook in 1774 discovered the Isle of Pines. Pale bark — thick, given to peeling in papery layers, and virtually fireproof — identifies the niaouli, a relative of the eucalypts; death has stripped the small evergreen leaves from this tree. North of Nouméa, niaouli scrub covers the hillsides. Extremely durable in seawater, the timber serves local boat builders; it also yields oil, popular for head colds. Since the niaouli is native to New Caledonia, its name has come to distinguish the island-born. Caledonians claim it as "national" tree and the flightless cagou, unique to the island, as "national" bird. Normally the cagou hatches only one egg a year; slow afoot, it falls easy prey to dogs; today it approaches extinction.

across!" she marveled. But he was only assisting the small outboard engine that powered the craft. As we gathered way, he dropped to the deck again.

Torrential rains ended our journey at Hienghène. In the dry season we could have pushed on north to Cook's landfall at Balade and then completed a circuit of the island.

Disturbing reports of a hurricane hurried us back to Nouméa. Racing the storm, we boarded a plane for Ouvéa, an atoll 63 miles east of the mainland.

Dependencies of New Caledonia include the Loyalty Group—Ouvéa, Maré, Lifou,—and the Isle of Pines. Although on clear days you can see the Loyalties from New Caledonia mountaintops, Cook never discovered

MICHAEL E. LONG, NATIONAL GEOGRAPHIC STAFF (ABOVE), AND JACK FIELDS

them. The honor went to William Raven, another sea captain, who reported the islands as an incidental discovery during a Pacific voyage in the 1790's.

On Ouvéa Madeleine and I stayed in one of the native-style round huts belonging to Moasen Youssef, an Arab trader, at Fayaoué, the main settlement.

"I left the Yemen with my father when I was 11 years old, and I don't ever want to go back to stay," Moasen told us. "I was on ships for 27 years and I've been around the world three times. I'm satisfied. I'd still like to make the pilgrimage to Mecca before the end of my days, and perhaps have another look at the Yemen. But I'll return to Ouvéa, my adopted land."

The busy throng that stopped at Moasen's little store included few men—most of them are usually away, working in the mines or the factories on New Caledonia.

Consequently they neglect island gardens, but nobody starves. Fish abound in the lagoon, and the coconut grows in such abundance that Moasen, again and again, served us "millionaire's salad," the tender shredded growth cut from the heart of the palm. For each meal he had to sacrifice a grown tree. We wound up staying long enough to eat a lifetime's ration, for immediately after our arrival Hurricane Glenda canceled air service for eight days.

As the storm moved closer, we quickly explored the narrow island. At one point

153

only about 500 yards separated the ocean-battered east coast from the twelve-mile beach of white sand that borders the western lagoon.

A New Caledonia postage stamp pictures Ouvéa's most impressive sight: the cliffs called Lékine, where waves had cut deep limestone grottoes before the island was lifted up from the sea eons ago. The columns that formed in the caves now stand exposed under the vaulted overhang of the cliffs like the pillars of a great natural cloister.

In previous storms tidal waves have swept right over parts of Ouvéa, but Glenda sheered off to the south, and we left in peace.

NEW CALEDONIA made a late bid for the tourist trade. As recently as 1959 fewer than 900 tourists stopped at the island. In 1966 some 7,000 travelers arrived, many to watch the South Pacific Games at Nouméa. For this event, held every three years on a different island, athletes gather in friendly rivalry from all over the Pacific.

Though New Caledonia attracts travelers today, it once repelled them. The French, who took possession of the island in 1853, declared it a penal colony ten years later. After the failure of the Paris insurrection of 1871, France sent some 3,900 political prisoners to the Isle of Pines and to Maré.

While Madeleine returned to Sydney, I flew to the Isle of Pines with National Geographic Society picture editor Michael E. Long, crossing a 27-mile strait of shoals and coral banks. The airfield, set in inland scrub country, gave little indication of the beauty to come, but when a bus took us to the beachside hotel Mike paused in wonderment.

"Look at that beach!" he exclaimed. "I can't believe there's anything so white."

Along the dazzling beach, white as talc and almost as soft, stand casuarinas and coco palms. The island's pines, spiring 100 to 150 feet, with branches no longer than 6 feet, crest the low hills and fence the rockier shores. They crowd the numerous offshore islets with a bristling growth.

"That island's just like a hairbrush," Mike said, and our host laughed.

"That's the name of it: Îlot Brosse," he said. He was Albert Hogan, an Australian so long resident in New Caledonia he gave his own name a French pronunciation.

We were staying in clean, roomy, thatched cabins at the Kuniékaa hotel. Half a mile away, the abandoned prison provided grim contrast to the freedom and beauty of the island. After nearly a century the brick buildings still seemed to brood with menace.

"It's hard to believe people with ordinary feelings could do this to other people," Albert said when he took us there. Doors stood open; pigs rooted in the narrow cells where prisoners had served their sentences, watched by a guard stationed on a platform in the center of the yard.

We found the village of Vao much more pleasant, its people proud and happy, its children irresistible. Near the shore, fishermen worked at their canoes, getting ready for the night and its catch.

With Albert and a couple of other new friends, we fished one night a mile or so from shore under a moon that threw circled rainbows against hurrying clouds. In short order we caught 38 fish: rock cod, New Caledonian dorado, groper, and one or two I could not identify. Some weighed as much as 12 pounds.

On other days, we strolled onto the lawn that separated dining room from beach and enjoyed *pétanque,* a game like bowls, but played with baseball-size metal balls we threw rather than rolled. Sometimes we sat in wordless communication with the carver who was cutting stylized hands and faces of ancestor guardians into heavy gateposts for the Kuniékaa's new entrance.

These quiet pleasures never palled. All too soon Mike had to move on to one new country and I to another. As always when a Pacific island recedes into ocean-smothered silence, I felt an inexpressible sadness—a sadness that ends only when new islands rise above the horizon.

Behind their battalion flag, troops of the Infanterie de Marine *in battle dress march briskly in Nouméa to commemorate the annexation of New Caledonia by France on September 24, 1853. Admitted to the French Republic in 1946, the Territory today elects its own Assembly and sends two representatives to the Parliament in Paris.*

JACK FIE

CHAPTER EIGHT

NEW HEBRIDES

Fragments of Green on a Sapphire Sea

"VOLCANO! Dead ahead! There's a volcano erupting!" The excited voice of the airline steward abruptly ended the pleasant reverie I had fallen into while gazing down at dark green islands in the New Hebrides. As the pilot banked in a wide circle, I stared transfixed at the most awesome fire I had ever seen. As a bomber pilot for the Royal New Zealand Air Force in World War II, I had seen some big ones — oil refineries — but they were insignificant compared to this seething shaft of lava and incandescent ash.

"The island of Lopevi," our pilot said to me later. "It must have gone up this morning. As the plane approached, I opened the cockpit window and felt the heat. I've flown among volcanoes for a dozen years, and this is the most spectacular eruption I've seen."

Below, the perfect cone of the island, its upper slopes ablaze, reared 4,755 feet from a seagirt base three miles across. Between the lava flows, small green pockets seemed untouched. Perhaps, I thought, such places offered sanctuary to the inhabitants of Lopevi. Later, I learned that all 250 of them had fled their island.

At last the pilot swung away toward Vila, capital of the New Hebrides. Below, long

Hurtling headfirst from a 65-foot jungle tower, a land diver proves his courage in a feat seen only on Pentecost Island. Vines knotted around the performer's ankles will break his fall abruptly at the moment his head touches the ground.

DAVID ATTENBORO

streaks of orange-colored ash lay on the sea. Islands slid beneath us: Epi, the Shepherds, Nguna, Emau, and Pele: fragments of green scattered on the sapphire sea.

I could not hope to visit more than a few of the 72 islands and islets of the New Hebrides, though their scattered 80,000 inhabitants have a fascinating variety of cultures.

Roughly central, the port of Vila, on the island of Efate, seemed the place to start. From there I would fly north to Malekula, where hills and mountains harbor the strange tribesmen called Big Nambas, and south to volcanic Tanna and then to quiet Aneityum.

Miss Tessa Franklin—then administrative secretary of the Chamber of Commerce at Vila, now Mrs. John Fowler—approved my choice. "The islands have a quality different from other South Pacific groups," she said. "Their beauty, to me, is not quite real; perhaps I can put this down to seeing them through a faint volcanic haze. But the most interesting thing is the people themselves. They vary from island to island—the Tannese especially are different.

"You remember *Tales of the South Pacific,* the book and the movie. Well, author James Michener got a lot of his characters right here. And some of his stories. It's a rich field. There'd be something over 3,000 Europeans here now, several hundred people from other island groups, and a few Vietnamese."

Until recently the population of the New Hebrides was on the decline. In the early 19th century sandalwooders depleted the aromatic wood in Fiji, then turned to the New Hebrides, the Loyalties, and New Caledonia. When sandalwood again became scarce, many ship captains began recruiting laborers for plantations in Fiji and Australia.

These "blackbirders," as they were called, rounded up some recruits by force, sank canoes at sea and "rescued" the struggling men and women, or simply induced them to come of their own accord. Others they bought from chiefs or relatives, paying with tobacco, muskets, mirrors, or beads.

Isolation had kept these islanders vulnerable. Diseases new to them—smallpox, influenza, whooping cough—killed thousands. John G. Paton, a Presbyterian missionary

from Scotland who arrived in the New Hebrides in 1858, recorded that some captains deliberately carried people suffering from measles. Recruiters could expose captives to the infection before allowing them to return to their people. At times, Paton wrote, the blackbirders seemed motivated by sheer malice.

"I am ashamed to say that these Sandalwood and other Traders were our own degraded countrymen," Paton wrote. "... A more fiendish spirit could scarcely be imagined, but most of them were horrible drunkards, and their traffic of every kind amongst these Islands was, generally speaking, steeped in human blood."

Disease and native muskets, clubs and arrows killed many missionaries in the New Hebrides. Paton accused both recruiters and traders of creating hostilities that led to murder. A few literate captains defended recruiting as a means of introducing island people to the benefits of civilization.

In recruiting days the islands were a no man's land between British influence in the Solomons to the northwest, and French influence in New Caledonia and the Loyalties to the southwest. The two nations in 1887 set up a Joint Naval Commission, and in 1902

In full flight, a diver plunges to a slope cleared of stones and spaded to cushion his landing. Play in the rickety tower will ease the jolt when lifelines stretch taut—injuries rarely occur. Below, friends rush to help pick up a grinning jumper.

EDWARD K. SHELMERDINE (BELOW) AND IRVING JOHNSON

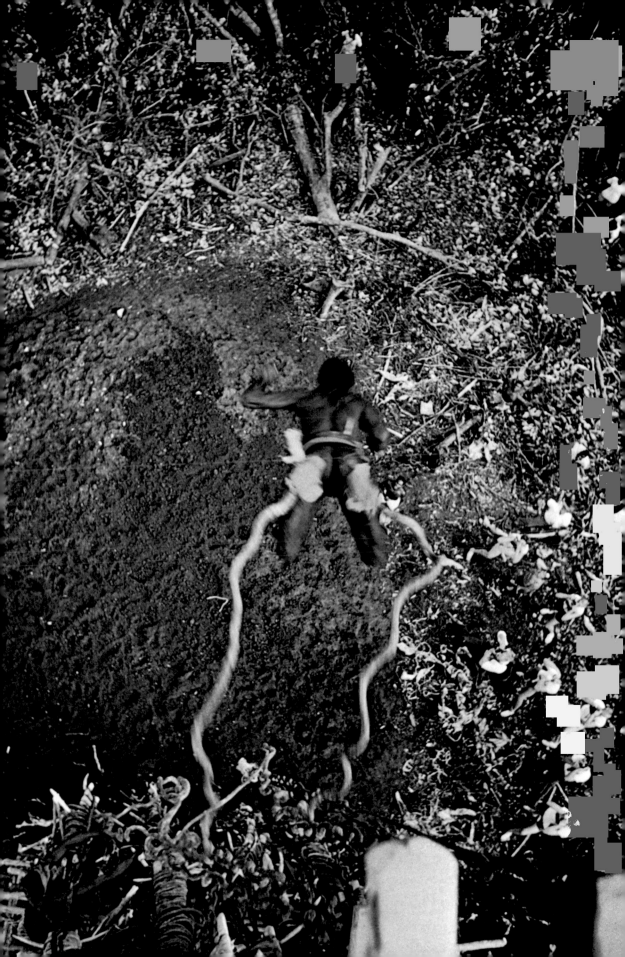

From the harbor town of Vila on Efate Island, French and British commissioners administer the New Hebrides. Miliciens *in red caps enforce the law with Britannic colleagues. At the British Resident's jetty on Iririki Island, crewmen like John Tapasei man a launch for runs to the capital.*

appointed Resident Commissioners. In 1906 they signed the convention that established the Anglo-French Condominium that continues today.

In Vila, I talked with Brett Hilder, artist, author, aviator, and ship captain, about this divided rule. "It's an unusual kind of administration," he told me, "not overgoverned or overregulated, since the French and English must usually come to a compromise. Most residents like the Condominium because it gives them more freedom. It's a bit frustrating, perhaps, for the officials."

A Frenchman sums it up with a shrug: "It's Napoleon versus Lord Nelson."

Condominium buildings and vessels fly two flags of equal size, one French and one British; I watched one of the launches pull in to the jetty, its Melanesian sailors standing at attention. In this sheltered harbor the few larger ships still lie in the roads, discharging by lighter their cargoes of cars and tractors, building materials, clothing, canned or frozen foods. But a new deepwater wharf will simplify matters.

Tax-shelter advantages under British law are bringing "offshore" companies, mostly Australian, to Vila; and officials foresee new revenues—perhaps even $300,000 a year— to support hospitals and education. "There's been more change here in the last 10 years than in the past 50," says one resident, "more in the last 3 than the previous 10."

Copra remains a major export; but profit margins shrink, and more and more growers are putting fine Charolais cattle from France to grazing under the palms. Choice steaks will sell quickly in Nouméa.

The boom in New Caledonia means a labor shortage here, and employers talk of getting more men from the Gilberts; but it also means more money in circulation. Men—and girls—come home with cash to pay for shirts or tea services or even cars. But older styles have not disappeared from streets where the cackling of hens can be heard in mid-morning.

A smiling woman in a short lace-bound Mother Hubbard, her hair bleached red with lime, nodded to me as she walked past. She carried a short stem of bananas in one hand, a string of live coconut crabs in the other.

"Market he stop long where?" I asked. I was not sure she would understand me for,

while New Hebrides pidgin is allied to the New Guinea pidgin I speak, it differs greatly in vocabulary. But she smiled and pointed her chin in the direction from which she had come. A little way on, I found a line of women sitting comfortably on the ground, selling sweet potatoes, coconuts, and tropical fruit. I bought a hand of bananas, a papaya melon, and a shell necklace.

Of the town's three hotels, I had chosen the Vate. In one corner of the lobby stood an eight-foot length of log slotted and hollowed by Ambrym islanders as a signal drum. Above the slot a carved, hollow-cheeked face seemed to regard me with dislike. Flanking the doors and on stair landings stood more carvings, some in wood, some cut into fibrous tree-fern trunks.

Many of the figures carried pig tusks mounted like horns or mustaches on the

161

carved black faces. Some of the tusks had developed into double spirals during the pig's lifetime, like springs of ivory. On a number of Melanesian islands men breed pigs mainly for their tusks, knocking out the tooth that normally would grind against the tusk in the lower jaw and wear it down. The tusk grows and curves unchecked, often penetrating the cheek. The owner prizes such an animal highly, frequently even more than a wife. Some of the pigs are sacrificed at initiation rites and for funeral feasts.

Many New Hebrideans have developed amazing rituals. On thickly forested Pentecost Island, men — and boys as young as eight — prove their courage by land diving, plunging headfirst from a tower of small vine-lashed tree trunks. Long springy lianas are knotted around the jumper's ankles and fixed to a collapsible diving platform that juts from the tower. When it seems the hurtling jumper must crash to the ground, his weight snaps slender boughs that support the outer edge of the diving board. The collapsing platform slows his fall, and the tautening vines stop him abruptly at the instant his head touches the spaded earth. Despite the severe jolts absorbed by the jumpers, few are injured. The height of the leaps, traditionally performed at yam-planting time, varies from 25 feet to 80 feet or more.

A strange rite survives among some 400 Big Nambas in northwest Malekula. The men barter pigs and yams for wives, and a husband may reward a hard-working, virtuous wife with a costly, secret ritual. At the ceremony, a selected tribesman knocks out two of the wife's front teeth, an honor coveted by Big Nambas women.

As late as the 1930's these people warred among themselves almost constantly, and the victors often devoured slain enemies. But the last report of cannibalism came some twenty

Erupting unexpectedly, Karua submarine volcano discharges white steam and black masses of ash, cinders, and lava bombs from three vents off Tongoa, February 22, 1971. Ten days later visitors explore still-warm Karua Island, noting a stench of sulphur and seawater too hot to touch. On the skyline rises the classic cone of Lopevi.

years ago. Now the villages remain peaceful. Western disease killed many Big Nambas; in the past twenty years about a thousand have come down to the coast to seek a better life and an education for their children.

I went to Malekula and set out to visit those Big Nambas in the mountaintop village of Amok. For two days I climbed in drenching rain. Finally, the infection of a bad cut on my leg forced me to turn back. I hope to return someday, for though the Big Nambas have had much contact with outsiders, they are among the very last people of the Condominium still unaffected by Western ways.

The first European to see the New Hebrides, Pedro Fernández de Quirós, landed on Espíritu Santo in 1606. Captain Cook, however, was first to touch at most of the islands. Some of the New Hebrides' past—and its present—is preserved in Vila's cultural center, which houses 6,000 books in French and English, as well as a collection of New Hebrides birds, insects, and artifacts.

I drove to Forari along a road that skirted miles of white-sand beaches and sheltered jade-green pools bordered with coconut palms, casuarinas, pandanus palms, and acacia bushes laden with yellow blooms. There I saw manganese mining, the only heavy industry in the New Hebrides. The process at Forari is one of stripping away earth to expose shallow ore, digging the ore, washing it, cooking it with coke, and loading the resulting manganese monoxide into ships for the manufacture of alloys, mostly in Japan.

At Forari's harbor, on the east coast of Efate, I met Jean Brébion, a lithe and lively master mariner retired from the French merchant service.

"I would rather live in the New Hebrides than any other place on earth," he told me. "Here is Paradise. The *habitants* are the finest of people; you need never lock your house to keep out more than the wind and the rain. I have swallowed the anchor."

His little house on top of the hill overlooks the anchorage. Not far away stands a church shared by Catholics and Protestants. A fire-extinguisher casing, World War II surplus, serves as church bell. Inside the hexagonal building, individual seats, round and backless, spring from the floor in a honeycomb pattern. Thus Catholics can face their altar for worship and, in the following hour, Protestants their pulpit and communion table.

On Tanna, my next objective, live about 70 percent of the pagans in the New Hebrides. Early in this century missionaries believed they were winning the island for Christ, but in the last 25 years Tannese shaped a religion of their own. In varying ways, three cults worshiped a god called Jon Frum, reincarnation of an older deity. Cultists proclaimed that Jon Frum would usher in a time of plenty.

JACK FIELDS

Wearing pig tusks worth a fortune and a train of palm fronds, Chief Tofor of Fanla village on Ambrym carries a nul nul, *or club of rank. Left, before a log gong, his followers converge in a dance of joy for the upgrading of a chief—in this case, the Duke of Edinburgh. Visiting the New Hebrides in 1971, Prince Philip was given a name meaning "Great Chief of All the Islands."*

JACK FIELDS

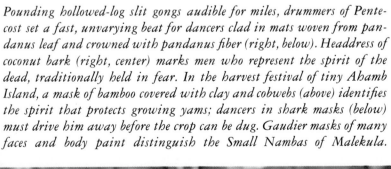

Pounding hollowed-log slit gongs audible for miles, drummers of Pentecost set a fast, unvarying beat for dancers clad in mats woven from pandanus leaf and crowned with pandanus fiber (right, below). Headdress of coconut bark (right, center) marks men who represent the spirit of the dead, traditionally held in fear. In the harvest festival of tiny Ahamb Island, a mask of bamboo covered with clay and cobwebs (above) identifies the spirit that protects growing yams; dancers in shark masks (below) must drive him away before the crop can be dug. Gaudier masks of many faces and body paint distinguish the Small Nambas of Malekula.

Bulging eyes and curved pig tusks ornament a headdress shaped from a tree-fern trunk and worn by initiates into men's fraternities on Malekula island. All four sides show the same face. Carved to stand before a miniature house, the figure at top left signifies social rank purchased with pigs. Vegetable paste molded over a skull (center) reproduces a dead man's likeness. In one of several rites performed to help yam vines grow, young islanders wear a painted mask (bottom) with hair of bleached banana-trunk fiber. Wooden puppets at right play roles in a myth portraying death and resurrection.

Money should be thrown away, gardens neglected, pigs slaughtered; followers would need none of these.

Between 1941 and 1952 police arrested 150 of these "messengers" of Jon Frum, as the prophets called themselves. Some were jailed, others banished. But the movement gained ground, especially when American troops arrived on Efate and Espíritu Santo with enormous quantities of goods.

All through Melanesia, the impact of civilization with its material wealth fostered new religions that promised the coming of a god or a messiah. At least 70 cults, most of them moribund now, preached the advent of a Heaven-sent cargo of consumer goods.

ARRANGED to visit the village of Sulphur Bay, then headquarters of the most aggressive of the Jon Frum movements. A Fijian friend, Manueli Balasaga, and an American archeologist accompanied me. By Land-Rover we followed a road that led through forest and acacia scrub to the Yasur volcano. Beneath its fires, some cultists believe, Jon Frum commands an army of 5,000. Others believe he rules a village there.

We skirted the base of the volcano to Sulphur Bay, where a beach of dark sand bordered a narrow, grassy plain. Red-painted wooden crosses, fences, and crude models of aircraft—symbols of the movement—stood eerily in the volcanic haze. Leaf huts rose near the foot of the hills and along the beach. The women retreated as we approached; the children kept a wary distance. Under a banyan near the beach villagers had erected a small shelter, and here we waited for Nampas, leader of the Tanna movement.

After an hour, he came down from a hilltop garden wearing a mud-stained lava-lava. With Manueli and a villager interpreting, he told us that adherents met every Friday at the shelter, and that Jon Frum appeared in person and spoke to the people. From others, I have heard that Nampas only received messages sent by Jon Frum.

Now Nampas has died, and some of the men who worshiped Jon Frum are seeing the ways of the West through jobs on New Caledonia. Some have returned to the missions; some, as the local phrase puts it, "to custom"—to ancestral ways.

Yasur, at least, is constant. Manueli and I climbed its boulder-strewn slopes. A sound as of distant cannon heralded a fiery barrage of rocks. Most fell back into the crater; a few bounded onto the slopes. Wind-blown smoke eddied and whirled, revealing glimpses of the crater's depths. Gas constricted our breathing. I felt glad enough to come down.

We drove on to Port Resolution. Here, in 1774, Cook had sailed into a small inlet and found that it opened into sheltered water. He named the harbor for his ship. A century later, shallowing and silting left the port virtually useless as an anchorage.

Tanna disturbed me with the rumblings of its volcano and the rebellions of its men, but most New Hebrideans inhabit happy islands. I flew to Aneityum on an interisland plane that landed on a sandy islet. Passengers walked a few yards to a tender with an outboard engine for the 15-minute run to Aneityum's shelving beach.

I had a lunch of fried rice with Artie Krafft, sawyer, mechanic, and storekeeper. When I asked if he were the only European on the island, he shook his head. "There's another fellow here," he said, "round the back of the island." Some months later, I learned, the man had died. Artie's neighbor was gone.

Along the beach, ragged but brightly dressed men, women, and children sang songs and laughed, delighted by the entertainment of the plane's arrival. Few toiled at anything but subsistence gardening, and fewer still cared. I decided that all the island had to offer was sunshine and happiness.

Sunshine and happiness, though, I hold infinitely more precious than the sandalwood that traders once took from Aneityum. And contentment is infectious. I have found few places on earth more pleasant—or more intriguing—than the New Hebrides.

Lava fountain flings scarlet spray within the crater as Mount Yasur, on eastern Tanna, hisses and rumbles in continuous but feeble eruptions. Golden-hot swirls may reach 2,000° F. Ash blows from the summit, with the delicate filaments of volcanic glass known as "Pele's hair."

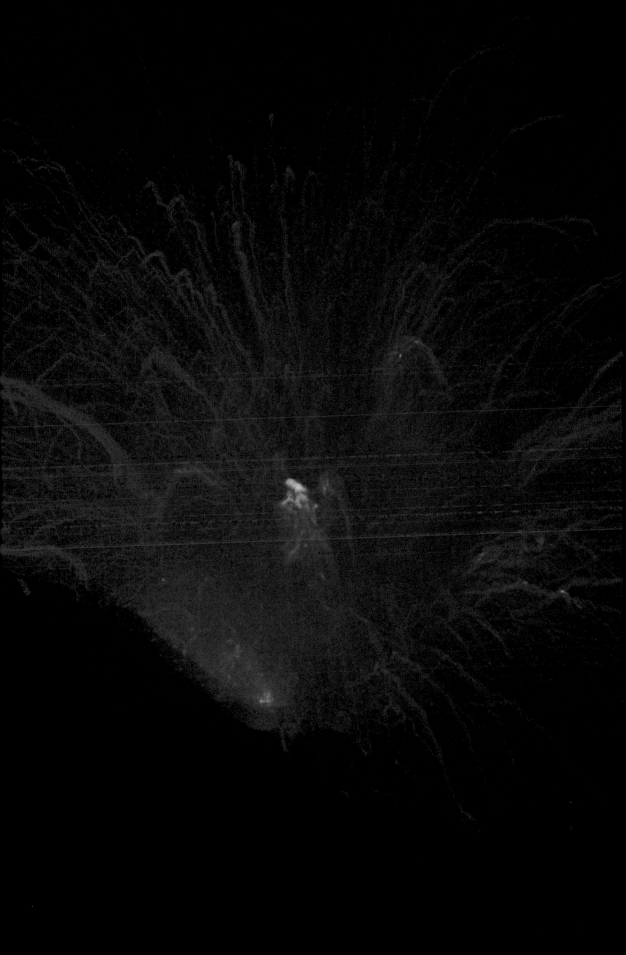

CHAPTER NINE

THE SOLOMONS

Memories of War Linger in the "Golden Isles"

POINCIANAS AND PALMS, tulip trees and weeping figs cast welcome shade as I strolled the main street of Honiara, burgeoning capital of the British Solomon Islands Protectorate and home to some 13,000 people. Modern concrete-and-glass buildings, housing the Secretariat and High Court of the Western Pacific, gleamed on wide lawns between the bay and the grassy ridges that hem in the town. Out on the reef, two brown-skinned women in bright print dresses poked about looking for shellfish.

Britain's largest Pacific holding, the Protectorate reaches in a double line of islands across 900 miles of the Coral Sea. From Honiara the Western Pacific High Commission administers the Solomons—and also looks after the British interest in the New Hebrides, 800 miles to the southeast.

Entering the town's commercial center, I passed the seafront Hotel Mendana, which workmen were busily expanding and modernizing. Here a few detached rooms represented Honiara's oldest and one of its most widely used architectural styles—modified World War II military hut. On nearby Point Cruz dock workers emptied small trading schooners of copra garnered at dozens of small

Dugout canoes glide to market on Malaita Island's Takwea River, a narrow stream that harbors crocodiles. Once weekly, a flotilla of some two dozen of these tiny craft sets out with fish fresh from the Lau lagoon (background).

Guadalcanal:
Grim relics evoke
World War II

Morning glory veils artillery shells at Hell's Point, where more than 25 years

earlier U.S. Marines hurled back Japanese troops in savage fighting. The

ordeal of Guadalcanal began on August 7, 1942, when some 10,000 men of the

U.S. 1st Marine Division landed on Red Beach to open a six-month campaign

that broke the back of Japan's mighty Pacific offensive and turned the tide of

war. Today, boys balance on a Japanese anti-aircraft gun near a blazing picnic

fire on the historic beach. Dense growth envelops the wreckage of a

U.S. Sherman tank used by training units after fighting ended on the island.

islands and remote bays throughout the Solomons. Not far away, an overseas copra vessel waited to carry the export to England, Japan, and Australia.

The day before, I had gazed from a porthole of an interisland plane at the faint, mellowed outlines of trenches and redoubts. A few shell-torn and sea-ravaged landing craft still encrusted the beaches — scores of others had gone for scrap.

As I studied these vestiges of war, I imagined I could hear the clash of arms on the plain, the deep thunder of naval guns offshore, and the whine of warplanes around me, for this was the island of Guadalcanal, where the Allies had stalled the mighty Japanese offensive and changed the course of the Pacific war. My plane dipped to a landing at Henderson Field.

I found that the war remains real to the people of Honiara — sometimes uncomfortably so. Gardeners' spades turn up shrapnel, cartridges, rifles, and even unexploded shells. In the summer of 1967 a British bomb-disposal team, working to extend the runway of Henderson Field, peeled back 25 years of tropical growth and uncovered 11,000 bombs and shells, most of them from stockpiles abandoned by the Allies. Tons of explosives still lie buried in a 270-acre area near Honiara, awaiting careful removal as the town expands.

Japanese troops went ashore on Guadalcanal on July 4, 1942, and on its northern plain began to build an airbase that could threaten the long chains of islands to the southeast, and eventually Australia itself. But though the Japanese laid out Henderson Field, the Allies named it and used it.

On August 7, some 10,000 men of the U. S. 1st Marine Division splashed ashore in Operation Watchtower, first great American amphibious assault of the Pacific war. The Marines met almost no opposition in the landing and quickly occupied the airfield. But the following day enemy planes forced U. S. transports to stop unloading supplies. That night a Japanese force of eight ships slipped past a destroyer patrol off nearby Savo Island, sinking four Allied cruisers and two destroyers and damaging other key ships.

After the savage attacks, Allied naval forces withdrew. Soon Japan began a bitter campaign to push the Marines off Guadalcanal. From the island of Bougainville, troop and supply ships of the "Tokyo Express" sped down The Slot, a wide seaway that splits the Protectorate into two chains of islands. Japanese planes began almost daily bombing runs over Guadalcanal. For six months the Marines, later reinforced by infantry soldiers, endured a nightmare of almost constant bombardment from sea and air, blood-chilling banzai charges by screaming enemy soldiers, drenching rains, malaria, and a plague of biting and stinging insects.

The ordeal of Guadalcanal ended in victory for the Allies in February, 1943. By then some 60 ships had died in deadly battles off the north shore of the island, giving that stretch of water the name Iron Bottom Sound.

An Air Age capital — youngest in the Pacific — Honiara sprang up around wartime

World War II hero, Sgt. Maj. Vouza served as a scout for U. S. Marines on Guadalcanal. Seized by the Japanese, he refused to reveal American positions though tied to a tree and bayoneted repeatedly. Many Solomon Islanders, fiercely loyal to the Allied cause, distinguished themselves in battle. Bloody Ridge (opposite), still creased by a wartime road used by Marines, saw furious fighting in the struggle for Guadalcanal. Once a runway for fighters and bombers, Henderson Field (background) now serves commercial flights.
DAVID MOORE, BLACK STAR

Quonset huts built on Point Cruz west of Henderson Field. In an earlier seaborne age, Tulagi was capital of the Solomons, chosen because of the sheltered harbor between its tiny islet and the hills of Nggela Island in the Florida Group. But the war destroyed Tulagi. Today it serves mainly as a repair center for government boats that carry passengers and cargo among the islands.

Honiara takes its name from the native description of the Point Cruz area, *Naho-ni-ara,* which means "facing the east and south-east wind." Here, Alvaro de Mendaña, discoverer of the Solomons, raised a cross and claimed the island for Spain.

To their surprise, the Spaniards found the interior of this island of "many savannahs and bare mountains" heavily populated. A shore party climbed into the hills and saw that "more than thirty villages, of ten and twenty houses and more, could be counted within a league and a half of road."

The "Indians," as Mendaña's men called the Solomon Islanders, were sometimes

U. S. Marines on Bougainville advance through jungle so dense that snipers could lurk only yards away. By March, 1944, Marines and infantry had secured the vital Cape Torokina area, last major objective in the Solomon Islands.

friendly, more often hostile. On Santa Isabel they were "differently coloured ... some are black, and some are fair. . . ." On Guadalcanal, named by the explorers for a town in Spain, the people were "more robust and blacker," with "better villages and houses."

Inca tales of islands of gold 600 leagues to the west of Peru had inspired Mendaña's voyage. He sailed from Callao, Peru, in November, 1567. The following year, on February 7, he anchored off Santa Isabel and from there set out to explore the neighboring islands.

Though Mendaña found no gold, rumors spread after his return to South America that the islands were a vast treasure house. Men talked of riverbeds of gold on Guadalcanal; imaginative minds linked the "golden isles"

Clutching a wooden war club, high priest Kunua sits with assistants in a sacred house on Foueda Isla.

Shell-inlaid model of a ceremonial canoe holds a black figure whose name remains a secret kept by priests and chiefs. Craftsmen on Ontong Java Atoll carved the driftwood idol at left. The sacred images at right, one bearing a war club, will stand until they rot; tribesmen must not touch them.

...ese pagans believe ancestral spirits dwell here.

to the wealth of King Solomon. The name Solomon Islands appeared in official reports, and eventually became fixed in history.

From the Hotel Mendana, I could see two of Mendaña's discoveries—the dark-green cone of Savo Island and the low hills of the Florida Island Group off the north coast of Guadalcanal. Mendaña also discovered Malaita, San Cristobal, and Choiseul. The northwest islands of Bougainville and Buka—once ruled by Germany, now administered by Australia as part of Papua New Guinea—and Vella Lavella, New Georgia, Rendova, and Kolombangara remained for later explorers.

In 1893 Great Britain declared a protectorate over the southern islands, extending her influence until 1900, when the present boundaries were complete.

Though Britons fill most senior official positions in the Solomon Islands, Australian influence is strong. I felt at home when making purchases, for Australian money is used exclusively throughout this British Protectorate. The bulk of the Solomons' imports comes from Australia—along with most of the planters and businessmen. But the Spanish are not forgotten—Mendaña's name appears everywhere.

Nor has Honiara forgotten one of its first residents, the late Kenneth Houston Dalrymple-Hay, formerly proprietor of the Hotel Mendana. Before the town existed, he served the Allied cause here as a Royal Australian Navy coast-watcher. He and others like him, hiding in Japanese territory months before the Marines arrived, reported enemy activity at great risk, and by their very presence helped encourage the islanders to believe that someday Allied forces would drive out the Japanese.

Many Solomon Islanders distinguished themselves in war. Sgt. Maj. Vouza, captured by a Japanese patrol, refused to reveal the position of American troops on Guadalcanal though he was tied to a tree and bayoneted repeatedly. Left for dead, he escaped—and gave information leading to the destruction of a large Japanese force before allowing medics to dress his wounds.

Vouza, who before the war headed the Santa Cruz Islands police force, was described by

DAVID MOORE, BLACK STAR

District Officer Hector MacQuarrie as "a magnificent specimen of humanity.... His build had the grand simplicity of perfection, the reserve, the control, which marks the work of the great Greek sculptors...." He had, MacQuarrie observed, "brilliantly bronze hair."

Melanesians come in astonishing variety in the Solomons. Skin ranges from blue-black to light tan, and features are sometimes heavy, sometimes finely chiseled. Not infrequently fair hair accompanies dark-brown skin.

A developing tropic ulcer on my leg sent me to the Honiara section of the Solomons Medical Department. There I learned of the massive effort to eradicate malaria by attacking the female *Anopheles farauti* — the mosquito that transmits the disease from an infected person to a well one.

The government, with the World Health Organization, is now spraying inside each house at six-month intervals, killing mosquitoes that might be carrying the infection. In the New Georgia Group and the Shortland Islands and on Savo and Guadalcanal, where

the program began, spraying greatly reduced the incidence of the disease.

A score of medical officers, the majority island-born, along with several score men and women trained as nurses, care for the health of an estimated 166,000 people in the Solomons. The Fiji School of Medicine had 14 islanders enrolled in 1971, including 1 studying hygiene and 2 trainees in laboratory technology. In New Zealand and Papua-New Guinea, Solomon Islanders have just begun to join the ranks of university graduates.

Distances and a scarcity of transport delay every form of development. This problem struck me particularly in the outlying islands that are Polynesian enclaves: Rennell, Bellona, Ontong Java Atoll, Sikaiana, Tikopia, Taumako, and Anuta. So few outsiders have visited them that authorities fear savage epidemics like the measles scourge that killed Pacific islanders by the thousand in the 19th century. To protect inhabitants from infection, the authorities at Honiara require ships to get permission before calling at some of these remote islands.

Boarding the small diesel vessel *Kwai,* I set out for Bellona, more than 100 miles south. Easily reached by air today, the harborless island was accessible then only by boat. As we anchored, early next morning, most of the 580 inhabitants gathered on the beach with half a year's accumulation of copra.

Passengers came off with the mail, leaping into outrigger canoes. Skillful paddlers took us ashore through heavy, drenching seas.

Bellonese who received letters answered them immediately, for the boat would not stay long. Several small girls settled themselves on the sand and wrote for two or three hours. Between sentences some reached for guitars or ukuleles; others occasionally raced down the sand to swim among the rocks.

The *Kwai* departed before nightfall, and as it headed north the islanders waved and shouted goodbyes. They would not see another boat for months. In the dark morning hours the *Kwai* anchored in Wanderer Bay, on Guadalcanal's southwest corner.

Some 30 miles to the northeast of Guadalcanal lies the hot, humid, densely wooded island called Malaita, most populous of the

Solomons. Though the whole group claims 11,500 square miles of land, Malaita, with 1,775 square miles, shelters some 51,000 Melanesians, nearly a third of the population. Some Malaitans, perhaps as many as 10,000, still worship ancestral spirits.

I accompanied Richard Turpin, then District Commissioner, Malaita, to the Lau lagoon, where island builders live. These industrious people transport sand, earth, and chunks of coral in canoes and on log rafts as fill for transforming sea shallows into real estate. On the mainland they cultivate taro, yams, pawpaw, leafy vegetables, bananas, and sugar cane. The women commute by canoe from their island houses to the gardens, and the men spend much of the day fishing.

We landed on an island called Tauba and I asked an English-speaking guide why his people took the trouble to build islands.

"The air is better to breathe out here," he told me. I had to agree. The day sparkled, freshened by a brisk wind and frequent showers. On the lagoon children bobbed in canoes with no more than an inch of freeboard; others trotted in my wake as I walked among houses newly rebuilt after a recent hurricane.

A wealth of seashells, lustrous, intricately patterned, washes ashore on Pacific beaches. Once homes for mollusks, these brilliant specimens range from the venomous textile cone (12) to the rare golden cowrie (31) prized by collectors.

Identifications: (1) Aulica (Aulicina) vespertilio, *bat volute; (2)* Cymatium nicobaricum, *nicobar triton; (3)* Polinices melanostoma, *black-mouthed moon; (4)* Tridacna crocea, *saffron giant clam; (5)* Haliotis asinina, *two donkey's ear abalones, placed together; (6)* Harpa ventricosa, *inflated harp; (7)* Mitra mitra, *episcopal miter; (8)* Patella stellaeformis, *star limpet; (9)* Charonia tritonis, *Pacific triton; (10)* Terebra subulata, *subulate auger; (11)* Aulica (Aulicina) vespertilio, *bat volute; (12)* Conus textile, *textile cone; (13)* Conus marmoreus, *marble cone; (14)* Trochus niloticus, *commercial trochus; (15)* Vexillum plicarium, *plicate miter; (16)* Nerita polita, *polita nerite; (17)* Ovula ovum, *egg cowrie; (18)* Pecten pallium, *mantle scallop; (19)* Trachycardium elongatum, *elongate cockle; (20)* Lima lima, *file clam; (21)* Rhinoclavis asper, *rough cerith; (22)* Strombus aurisdianae, *Diana conch; (23)* Cypraecassis rufa, *bull mouth helmet; (24)* Cypraea talpa, *mole cowrie; (25)* Angaria delphinus, *delphinula snail; (26)* Lambis chiragra, *chiragra spider; (27)* Latirus (Latirulus) turritus, *turreted spindle; (28)* Pleuroploca filamentosa, *filamented horse conch; (29)* Sunetta scripta, *inscribed sunetta; (30)* Oliva sericea miniacea, *orange-mouthed olive; (31)* Cypraea aurantia, *golden cowrie; (32)* Chicoreus carneolus, *murex; (33)* Sunetta scripta, *inscribed sunetta; (34)* Turbo argyrostomus, *silver-mouthed turban; (35)* Strombus luhuanus, *blood mouth conch.*

VICTOR R. BOSWELL, JR., NATIONAL GEOGRAPHIC ST

A great boar slept in a sty of coconut logs, sprawled alongside his feeding trough—an enormous clamshell. Women clad only in faded wraparound skirts sat under a veranda, weaving rough mats. To help bridge the language barrier, I held out a camera before asking, "May I take your picture?"

Immediately they looked anxious and ran away, but returned in seconds, smiling and wearing their best clothes. They were still barefoot, and a few remained bare-breasted, but these wore clean skirts with flower designs. Others had dressed in fresh print frocks.

Next day, I cruised Langalanga lagoon, passing one artificial island after another. I went ashore on Laulasi, wandering among its massed bamboo and palm-leaf houses. An island councilor named Francis Ferani

Off limits to females, a house for adolescents and bachelors stands on stilts beside an islet of coral blocks laboriously constructed for homesites by Malaitans who prefer to live on Lau lagoon. A bushman with a clamshell necklace puffs a pipe bought from a trade ship; woven reeds in a high priest's ear show he has completed a pagan ritual. Another bushman from mainland Malaita carries a machete, as all his tribesmen do, for protection and for hacking through jungle undergrowth.

introduced himself and acted as a guide.

He took me to a place where no women or children followed—indeed they did not even gaze after us. Here stood three large houses with peaked roofs and bold lettering on their gables: "Headmaster Ru Gola," "Headmaster Maemadama," "Headmaster

Mousi." These headmasters controlled not schools, but spirit houses for ancestor worship. They were the pagan priests; one, a short, rotund individual named Maemadama, stood prominently forward in a little crowd of men, wearing a short wraparound skirt, and a flower in his short-cropped hair. I asked his permission to enter the houses; with a little hesitation he complied.

Darkness closed in as I stepped through the narrow doorway, and I waited for my eyes to adjust before I explored. A collection of parcels, wrapped in leaves of the sago palm, occupied niches in the far wall.

"Skulls?" I asked Francis. He nodded.

I walked toward the grisly ancestral relics, but Francis halted me when the priest uttered a curt command. At my feet I noticed the

ashes of a recent fire and could tell that a large group had gathered there.

Francis left me near a tiny graveyard, where I crossed a channel to another part of the village occupied mainly by Christians. Pagans and Christians sometimes live side by side on the built-up islands. Most of the young people embrace Christianity, but aging priests still carry on the old rituals.

Near unused spirit houses I saw a church and school built of sago leaf. I commented on the houses to a Christian named Matebos, a man with ginger-colored hair and chocolate skin decorated with intricate tattoos.

"Oh yes, the spirit houses remain. But the bishop has thrown out all the devils."

"Yet I notice women seem barred from them still."

187

"Oh, the women. They don't come here. It's tabu." Obviously, some of the old influences remain.

I could have stayed on Malaita a long while, exploring forests bright with huge and brilliant butterflies. But the time had come to leave for New Georgia, in the Western District of the Solomons. The first leg of my flight took me back to Henderson Field, on Guadalcanal. Seats rarely go empty on inter-island flights. Businessmen, missionaries, government officials, and hospital patients vie for places on small Britten-Norman Islanders and de Haviland Doves.

FROM HONIARA we winged north, dodging storms. Eight or ten at once towered on the horizon. We flew low past Savo Island, then banked west toward the Russells Group. I left the plane at Munda, on New Georgia.

American visitors to the island may recall a Medal of Honor winner and the ballad of his self-sacrifice. Alone and wounded, he charged a pillbox to save his comrades. Thus, "to the everlasting glory of the Infantry lives the story of Private Rodger Young."

My first afternoon in Munda I walked along the shore and saw two girls bent over a canoe, struggling to lift out a protesting turtle that must have weighed 80 pounds. Farther on, I watched a fisherman spin a throw-net out over the reef so that it circled a school of finger-length fish. In the shallows a woman and a slim girl bathed with several children in water clear as air.

Later, I visited with Alec Wickham, once one of the world's most celebrated swimmers. He had grown up near Roviana lagoon in New Georgia, where the people had developed an overarm stroke that sped them through the water. As a young man, Alec and his brother left their Roviana home for school in Australia. There they introduced the new stroke to classmates. Eventually, as the Australian crawl, it changed swimming styles throughout the world.

A small dark man of 80, Alec stood 5 feet 7 inches. His face combined the European features of his father and the dark skin of his mother, a native of nearby Simbo Island.

We sat in gathering dusk while five geckos — small nocturnal lizards — stalked moths across the veranda ceiling. A canoe with a single paddler moved across the twilight-silvered lagoon between us and the dark islands. Leaping fish rippled the water.

Alec, who has since died, spoke quietly about Navy Lt. John F. Kennedy. In these waters, on August 5, 1943, two Gizo Islanders, scouts for coast-watcher Lt. Arthur Reginald Evans, had found the President-to-be on Olasana Island, with ten other survivors of Kennedy's wrecked PT boat.

After three days at Munda, I returned to Honiara and there talked with Ron Reece, a district manager for Lever Plantations, about a remarkable improvement in copra quality in recent years. Reece's plantation produces 500 to 700 pounds of first-grade copra to the acre. His formula: collecting nuts as soon as they fall, extracting the meat quickly, and sending it straight to the dryers, where it turns crisp and pearly gray. But no one has a formula to keep costs low and prices steady.

"The answer," said Ron, "has to be more mechanization, more efficiency. We use cattle to keep undergrowth down, not only so we can find the nuts, but also because brush competes with the palms for nourishment."

I asked about the future.

"The demand's permanent. Copra's here to stay. As for me, I came to the Solomons in 1948 and there's no place I like better."

Australian Eric Lawson, O.B.E., a Guadalcanal community leader, sees a significant trend toward progress as native attitudes rapidly become more modern. British authorities encourage the changes by promoting property ownership in Honiara and other settlements. Neat, well-kept houses attest the results, and gradually replace the barracks that once housed most native employees. The people of the Solomons come late into the 20th century, but they come with eagerness and adaptability. I think they may not be last when it ends.

Exchanging produce and gossip around a coconut palm, vendors and customers throng Malaita's Takwa market. Large orders of fish and vegetables sell for porpoise teeth and shell-disk strings. Australian shillings pay for smaller purchases.

CHAPTER TEN

NEW GUINEA

Islanders Leap From the Stone Age Into the 20th Century

AT THE MOUNT HAGEN AIRPORT in the Highlands of New Guinea a man wearing feathers stuck in a bark-cloth cap, and a heavy net apron caught at the waist by a bark belt, waited in line a step ahead of me. "Me like go long Goroka," he announced at the ticket window, waving his hand to include two companions who stood a little aside. They were his wife and daughter, both bare-breasted and wearing short, fringed skirts.

"Forty-one seventy," replied the European clerk as the tribesman produced three Australian twenty-dollar bills from the belt.

As I bought my own ticket, to the east-coast town of Lae, I thought how such a scene would have drawn amazed stares in almost any other country in the world. Here, it

brought hardly a glance. I was in the heart of New Guinea, where less than 35 years before tribesmen like the one waiting to board his plane lived in a Stone Age environment, fashioning axes of polished stone and warring almost continuously with neighbors. Now, frequently still in their Stone Age dress, they casually accept the convenience of the Air Age.

New Guineans have leaped into acceptance of the modern world, and "leap" is the appropriate word, for the whole of New Guinea

Beauty spots on a complexion of powdered red paint and pig grease help a New Guinea teenage belle attract suitors. After a carefree year or so of courtship, she will begin a life of hard work, leaving the prettying-up to her husband.

Forehead badge identifies a Wahgi clansman as a village leader appointed by Australian administrators. A masked Highlander wears cassowary plumage, and a tribesman puffs a cigar in a bamboo holder.

Plumes from birds of paradise shimmer on the heads of dancers at the Highlands sing-sing. Jeweled w

A time for dancing and parading in feathers and paint, the New Guinea Highlands fair, the year's biggest sing-sing, draws once-warring clans together. Old enemies become friends in the excitement of bicycle racing and log-sawing competition. To reach the fair, tribesmen walk over steep mountain trails for as long as three days, carrying a wealth of shells and plumes for display. In staging the event, the Australian administrators have a twofold purpose: to siphon off energies of fierce clansmen and, by introducing them to new crops and new ways, to help them in making the enormous leap from the Stone Age into the 20th century.

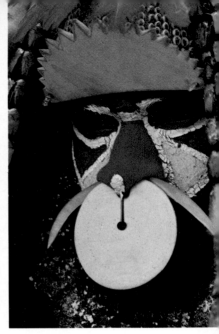

Grinning fairgoer admires himself in a mirror. Strings of scarab beetles frame the face of a painted clansman; shells pierce his nose.

ls, they sway and chant to a hypnotic rhythm rapped out on the opossum-skin heads of hourglass drums.

JOHN SCOFIELD, NATIONAL GEOGRAPHIC STAFF (UPPER RIGHT), AND JACK FIELDS

seems to be jumping, generating excitement, poised on the lip of time.

Second-largest island in the world, after Greenland, New Guinea divides into three political units that hold huge areas of mountain, jungle, coastal swamp, and off-lying isles. The western portion, the former Netherlands New Guinea, became part of Indonesia in 1963, its name changing to West Irian. Australia administers two areas jointly as a territory now called "Papua New Guinea." She took over control of Papua from Britain in 1906 and still administers it with the U.N. Trust Territory of New Guinea, once a German colony.

In Lae I looked up an old friend, Laurie Crowley, an Australian. When I first met him in 1949, Laurie was servicing planes on the island. Now he owned two air companies; his helicopters prowled distant valleys on charter to companies prospecting for minerals and oil. Often the puttering beat of the helicopters is more familiar to the people below than is the croak of the bird of paradise.

We marveled at this transition to the Air Age — Laurie remembered assistants who used to go off duty and paint their faces for a tribal sing-sing. Now shrieking turbo-prop aircraft are commonplace at Lae's airport, where I had arrived a few days earlier.

One of Laurie's pilots, Mrs. Bronwen Searle, flew me in a small high-winged Cessna monoplane to mountains in the northwest. Below us, as we crossed a spur of the Finisterre Range, the muddy, rain-swollen Markham River coursed a deep green valley in its rush to the sea. The first woman commercial pilot in New Guinea, Mrs. Searle flew with cool confidence above knife-edged spurs — skirting the precipitous cloud-veiled heights that shape the interior of this craggy island.

Looking down, I could see why the two and a half million people of the Territory speak more than 500 languages and dialects. Isolated by the mountains, clansmen in one valley often did not know of the existence of those in the next. Even tribes of only a few hundred developed languages of their own.

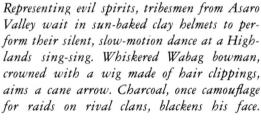

Representing evil spirits, tribesmen from Asaro Valley wait in sun-baked clay helmets to perform their silent, slow-motion dance at a Highlands sing-sing. Whiskered Wabag bowman, crowned with a wig made of hair clippings, aims a cane arrow. Charcoal, once camouflage for raids on rival clans, blackens his face.

Before the arrival of the first Australians in the early 1930's the Highlands remained a terra incognita to outsiders. Because of their very real fears, tribesmen kept to their home grounds. Over the whole of New Guinea endless wars and feuds had set a pattern for living. Sorcery was the spiritual reality, and some tribes were headhunters or cannibals.

Mrs. Searle and I headed for Bundi, a village on the flank of 14,793-foot Mount Wilhelm, highest peak in the Territory. But as we neared the gravel airstrip a heavy cloud slid down from the peak, its edge weaving and twisting. At times a scrap would whirl aside to offer a tantalizing glimpse of the village that clustered behind split-paling fences on a steep hillside below the approach to the strip. To the airplane goes the credit for opening up the interior — planes bring in everything from prefabricated schools to food.

Circling in the narrow valley, Mrs. Searle waited her chance. On the 15th pass, the gray curtain lifted and we scuttled under to land. A helicopter awaited us, and pilot Cliff Thornton quickly whisked us off the strip and up the narrowing valley. At heights as great as 8,500 feet, in gardens sloping as much as 55 degrees, women gouged the earth with pointed sticks, planting sweet potatoes, the basic food of the Highlander.

Pig fences ran up to the skies. Cliff pointed to one small herd tended by women. "Almost the only meat the people get is pork, so pigs are highly valued," he said. "All the more so because they are part of the bride-price a man pays when he is married. The pigs are looked after principally by the women, who sometimes suckle them. The animals are very tame, frequently following like pet dogs."

We headed for a drilling rig engaged in

195

testing the value of deep-buried copper deposits near Bundi. There, notched into a spur of the hill, the tiny heliport seemed hardly adequate for a landing, but the whole operation depended on this and six or seven similar pads in the Yandera Valley. Driller Thomas Lega and geologist Malcolm Castle showed me around the rig.

"With the chopper we can shift to a new site in two days," Tom said. "Just look at these steep slopes and you can imagine how long it would take without air transport."

Clouds closed in and chased us back to Bundi, where Mrs. Searle waited with the Cessna. There, scores of small boys, six to nine years old and all dressed in wraparound skirts cut from the same bolt of blue cloth, came running down from their mission school to watch us take off for the trip back to Lae. The bite of the propeller seemed to tear the clouds apart, and we were soon free in the lower valleys, with mountains towering on either side. I recalled the words of one early explorer, Italian Luigi Maria D'Albertis, that "...it is easier to ascend the highest peaks of the European Alps... than to cross an ordinary hill in New Guinea."

In the early 1930's, Australian patrol officers reached the great valleys of the Highlands, getting the earliest glimpse of some of the 600,000 tribesmen there. In 1933 Assistant District Officer James L. Taylor, joined by brothers Daniel and Michael Leahy, explored the headwaters of the Markham and Ramu Rivers in a series of air and land expeditions, finally pushing on to the cool green valley of the river called the Wahgi. Their discoveries disproved a belief held by Europeans in the Territory that the area was too barren and precipitous to support human life.

Where their maps showed only mountains, they found a high-walled valley. There, Michael Leahy recorded, "...green garden patches were a delight to the eye, neat square beds of sweet potatoes growing luxuriantly in that rich soil, alternating with thriving patches of beans, cucumbers and sugar cane."

In their first meetings with the people of the valley the explorers encountered broad-shouldered, bearded tribesmen carrying ten-foot spears and stone axes. They wore flowers and feathers in their hair and some had crescents of pearl shell in pierced noses. Some of the women began to wring their hands and one old man prostrated himself in front of the newcomers. Another raised his arm, drew a circle with his hand in the air, and made a sound like a motor. "They thought we had come out of the sky, dismounting that morning from the sun as it came over the eastern horizon, and that our coming had been heralded by the aeroplane," Taylor later wrote.

Further exploration of the Chimbu, Goroka, and other valleys followed the Leahy expedition to the Wahgi, and patrols penetrated deeper and deeper into the interior. Even today, first contacts are still being made with isolated peoples among the high ranges.

I determined to travel the Highlands by road. When the Cessna landed at Lae, I switched to a DC-3 to return to Mount Hagen; from there I could work my way to the coast again on the only road that leads all the way down from the Highlands, a route that evolved when disconnected mountain tracks were joined together.

Among majestic palms, a Kanganaman villager moves a food safe used to protect smoked meat and fish from rats. A carved post from the ruins of a spirit house stands beside a Sepik River hut built on stilts for the high-water season. Mount Hagen women plant corn with pointed sticks.

Another road, now under construction, will link the Highlands with Madang, a busy port on the north coast where cargo arriving by ship must now be flown inland.

At Mount Hagen I hired a minibus to reach the house of Robin Gray, a friend who grew coffee on a plantation about 50 miles down the valley. Groups of people walked the road, some carrying garden shovels — replacements for digging sticks. These Highlanders have green thumbs and, like many other Pacific islanders who live by gardening, they always find room for purely decorative plants.

They also decorate their persons more profusely, perhaps, than any other people. A man might wear a cap of black cassowary feathers, a cockade of blue and tan hawk wings, or a Prince Rudolph's blue bird of paradise, more brilliant than sapphire.

Women wear a variety of symbolic ornaments: clattering gold-lip pearl shells, cowrie shells, and lustrous bailer shells. The younger they are, the more shells they seem to carry. I noted that, a little north of Mount Hagen, handprints in white paint appeared on the bodies of some of the girls, and their noses were painted bright red, blue, or yellow.

Today, stores carry powdered paints in a much wider range of colors than the area's clays and plants provided. Other changes show more significant advances: A number of government and missionary schools and hospitals now serve the people; stores find a thriving market in soap, safety pins, canned soft drinks, and razor blades; and some tribesmen have become businessmen, turning to individual rather than clan rights in land, plantations, stock, and trucks.

I arrived at Robin's house after dark, and in the mountain chill we sat before a roaring fire in a room filled with bookshelves. In the morning, when mists pearled the valley where the Wahgi River coiled in great loops, I made the rounds with the overseer, and watched the laborers weeding coffee bushes

Bull's eye! Boys on New Britain Island play at killing wild pigs, hurling sharpened sticks at a rolling disk of banana stalk. Their sport equips them for the day they will go after real game. A tribesman (opposite) practices for a spear-thrusting contest, and a mother carefully binds the skull of her baby with bark cloth to shape the head into a fashionable elongated form.

198

JANE GOODALE (BELOW) AND ANN CHOWNING

laden with ripening berries. That dawn ushered in a typical Highlands day: cold fog in the morning replaced by brilliant sunshine, clouded skies after midday, heavy rains toward evening, and a still, clear night.

Later, Robin and I called on Kaibelt Diria, elected Member of the New Guinea House of Assembly. We found him supervising the building of a house for one of his four wives — he had divorced six others. Like most Highlands politicians, Kaibelt has opposed early independence for the Territory—a natural attitude. If pacification came late to the Highlands, economic development followed rapidly. For more than a century Lowlanders had seen development proceed slowly.

Other differences are apparent in the House. Papuans, more highly educated, are sometimes at odds with the wealthier and more numerous New Guineans; the people of Bougainville are sometimes at odds with all the rest. Despite these splits, however, self-government and independence seem real prospects today.

In March, 1971, the House of Assembly approved a plan for constitutional development and an approximate timetable for self-rule, and the Australian Government has accepted it. Self-government may come by 1976 or 1980 — no one can say when. Anyone can see that problems will remain: in finance, in trade, in education, in the perennial limitations of intractable land and weather.

The morning after my visit with Kaibelt, a truck driver and I set out for Lae with half a load of coffee to be shipped to Australia — the truck could not manage a full load in the rarefied air of the heights. The road cut through ice-cold mountain streams as we dropped into the Chimbu Valley. Not far to the north, the Bismarck Range rose spectacularly against the sky. In the Eastern Highlands, we crawled over Daulo Pass, 8,175 feet high, inching our way through thick mud. Friends had urged me not to miss the superb view from the pass, but the rain limited it to the sight of half a dozen black pigs grubbing for roots at the crest.

Two days after leaving Mount Hagen, we had crossed the 150 miles to Goroka, a bustling town in a wide valley holding scores of coffee plantations. Rainstorms had so cut into the road all the way to the coast that authorities imposed a ban on its use until crews

Slayer volcano, Mount Lamington lies dormant in the New Guinea
jungle. In 1951 the mountain hurled ash and rock over
90 square miles, taking 3,000 lives.

JOHN SCOFIELD, NATIONAL GEOGRAPHIC STAFF

Doll-like figure on stool typi-fies the fanciful art of the Trobriand Islands, off Papua' eastern tip. The happy, care-free people of the Trobriand have no fear of ancestral spirit, and carve only for ornament

"Cat's eye," the gemlike valve of a turban shell, glares from a fiber-crested mask worn in memorial dances for the dead on New Ireland, an island east of New Guinea.

Clay-covered skull copies the features and facial marking. of a deceased Sepik River tribesman. Human hair and cowrie-shell eyes add realism

could make repairs. To reach Lae, I abandoned the road and took to the air at Goroka.

In Lae I called on another friend, Australian-born Horace Niall, C.B.E., first Speaker of the New Guinea House of Assembly, a Councilor of the island's first university (the University of Papua-New Guinea, opened in 1966 in Port Moresby), and board member of many of the Territory's commercial enterprises. As Patrol Officer and District Commissioner, Horrie helped bring New Guinea forward from the Stone Age. And he also helped rebuild Lae after it had been left a shambles by bombing during World War II.

Back in 1949, I had accompanied Horrie on a waterborne expedition up the mighty Sepik River, a waterway in the northwest that twists and turns for more than 650 miles through some of the most remote parts of

the Territory. There, thick jungles and dense swamplands have yet to be fully explored. In the course of the expedition we encountered three isolated tribal groups, the Woga-mush, the Washkuks, and the May River people. We brought back more than 40 young men who were taught to speak pidgin and shown an ocean they never knew existed. In addition they learned how much better life could be without almost constant warfare. On their return the government appointed some as interpreters for their people.

Pidgin is a creole language with roots primarily in English, German, and Kuanua—the tongue of the Tolais of New Britain, a crescent-shaped island in the north that separates the Bismarck and Solomon Seas. Now the lingua franca of the Trust Territory, pidgin is spreading into Papua as well.

Human and animal symbolism mingles on a head-high shield fashioned not for war but for ceremony by people of the Sepik River country, once a haunt of headhunters. Limed grooves in an earthenware bowl form a whimsical face.

During my stay in Lae the headlines on the pidgin English newspaper *Nu Gini Tok Tok* (New Guinea Talk Talk) proclaimed "Painim Nupela Ples Long Bus," which, in more conventional spelling might read "Find Him New Fellow Place Long Bush," and is correctly translated "New Discovery in the Interior." The story concerned the finding of still another isolated group of people near Mount Bosavi in the Western District.

When a village leader gets his copy of the *Tok Tok,* sometimes months after publication, he usually reads it aloud to all the people. But, on the other hand, some buyers use the newspaper only to make wrappings for the long cigarettes New Guineans roll from home-grown tobacco.

From Lae, I flew by DC-3 to the southern coast—to Port Moresby, the administrative capital. While Lae is drenched with 180 inches of rain a year, Moresby's share averages only 40. In the dry season it often looks parched. The area's indigenous people, the Motu, were traders once, setting out in large sailing rafts made by lashing dugout hulls together. In annual trading expeditions lasting some three months, they went from village to village along the Gulf of Papua, bartering clay cooking pots for the sago flour they could not produce on their own drier acres. Some may have ventured as far as the wide estuary of the Fly River, which flows about 700 miles in a great arc from the Hindenburg Range.

World War II brought up-to-date machinery and job opportunities, so today's Motu works as a clerk, housepainter, fork-lift driver, or garage hand. When I first knew the

203

Its wings fluttering, a ribbon-tail bird of paradise trails twin feathers three feet long in a New Guinea aviary. A Victoria crowned pigeon carries a lacy crest. Curved mandibles of a New Guinea hornbill support a shell casque. In a vigorous courtship performance, a red-plumed bird of paradise displays his plumage to attract a mate.

port, the girls strolled the streets bare except for grass skirts, their skin covered with blue tattoos. Now, smartly dressed office girls walk briskly to their jobs, and only a few of those under 20 display more than a small symbolic tattoo on face or arms or legs.

Gabriel Keleny, a government officer stationed at Moresby, took me by car up the mountain road past Rouna Falls, where a hydroelectric project provides power for the growing town. New Guinea's combination of high rainfall and steep mountains offers impressive power potential.

Ahead rose a high escarpment where the Kokoda Trail begins its tortuous reach across the Owen Stanley Range to the north coast. On this trail in 1942, Australian troops turned back a Japanese advance that threatened Port Moresby, a vital point in the defense of Australia and in operations against enemy-held Rabaul on New Britain.

I had come to see rubber planting in the Sogeri district. Gabriel told me that the industry was undergoing a small revolution. "There is such a demand for seed of new, higher-yield imported varieties that a single seed is selling for around ten cents," he said. "Even at that, buyers outnumber sellers."

I could have dawdled for weeks in the cool and lovely atmosphere of the plantations: the green shade of the spaced trees, the silence, the thatched weighing sheds, the patterns of the chevroned bark, the cups balanced on bark-held pegs to catch the milky sap.

When I returned to Port Moresby I found a message in my hotel room: Francis Damien wished to interview me for the local radio station, which broadcasts in pidgin and English as well as Police Motu, the lingua franca of the Papuan coast. After the interview, I found that he was a Tolai from the Rabaul district, on New Britain's Gazelle Peninsula.

The Tolais have exemplified the changing face of New Guinea. Certainly they look to the future. The people derive income from trucking, copra, trade stores, and cooperatives that specialize in the processing and marketing of cacao beans. Local government councils have invested much tax revenue in schools and schoolteachers.

It was at Rabaul, where I flew to see the Tolais, that I ended my mission to Melanesia, a territory not easy to understand. Perhaps the only unifying factors for the diverse elements of Melanesia and Polynesia are the immutabilities of great distance and the remorseless sweep of the trade winds.

Distances remain, but now change sweeps the South Pacific—not with the slow, deep-rooted force that has molded the peoples' character over many generations, but with the swift, urgent energy of the 20th century. Islanders today are vigorously aware of the world beyond.

Now they are struggling to catch up, surging ahead at an amazing pace, in their ideas and beliefs, in their physical and intellectual environment. Nationhood emerges; the colonial era wanes. New patterns of regional cooperation begin to take shape across the seas of the blue sky.

Above all, the eternal stabilities of the ocean bind the islanders, as they bind me and my friend Maurice Shadbolt. For them as well as for us, wherever they go, the South Pacific will claim them, its call forever echoing and re-echoing in their ears.

Thatched haus tambaran, *or spirit house, stands 60 feet high in the East Sepik District. Tribesmen (left) shuffle to the beat of drums near the wood and fiber figure of an ancestral spirit. Dancers in spirit houses summon youths to view such secret images during manhood initiation rites.*

Index

Illustrations references appear in *italics*.

Additional References

For additional reading, you may wish to refer to the following NATIONAL GEOGRAPHIC articles: "Exploring New Britain's Land of Fire," Feb., 1961; "To the Land of the Headhunters," Oct., 1955; "New Guinea's Rare Birds and Stone Age Men," Apr., 1953; "New Guinea's Paradise of Birds," Nov., 1951, all by E. Thomas Gilliard. "Blowgun Hunters of the South Pacific," by Jane C. Goodale, June, 1966. "A Teen-ager Sails the World Alone," Oct., 1968, by Robin Lee Graham. "South Seas' Tonga Hails a King," by Melville Bell Grosvenor, March, 1968. "The Yankee's Wander-world," Jan., 1949, by Irving and Electa Johnson. "New Guinea Festival of Faces," July, 1969; "Journey into Stone Age New Guinea," Apr., 1969; both by Malcolm S. Kirk. "The Friendly Isles of Tonga," March, 1968; "Tahiti, 'Finest Island in the World,'" July, 1962; "The Islands Called Fiji," Oct., 1958; "Huzza for Otaheite!" Apr., 1962; "I Found the Bones of the Bounty," Dec., 1957, all by Luis Marden. "Land Diving With the Pentecost Islanders," Dec., 1970, by Kal Muller. "New Guinea: Netherlands and Australian," by John Scofield, May, 1962. "New Zealand's Cook Islands: Paradise in Search of a Future," Aug., 1967; "New Zealand: Gift of the Sea," Apr., 1962; "Western Samoa, the Pacific's Newest Nation," Oct., 1962, all by Maurice Shadbolt. "Captain Cook, The Man Who Mapped the Pacific," Sept., 1971; "In the Wake of Darwin's Beagle," Oct., 1969, both by Alan Villiers. "New Zealand, Pocket Wonder World," by Howell Walker, Apr., 1952.

Composition by National Geographic's Phototypographic Division, John E. McConnell, Manager. Printed and bound by Fawcett Printing Corp., Rockville, Md. Dust jacket printed by Lebanon Valley Offset Company, Inc., Annville, Pa. Color separations by Lanman Engraving Co., Alexandria, Va.; Beck Engraving Co., Philadelphia, Pa.; and Graphic Color Plate, Inc., Stamford, Conn., Progressive Color Corp., Rockville, Md. Cloth binding printed by The Lehigh Press, Inc., Pennsauken, New Jersey.

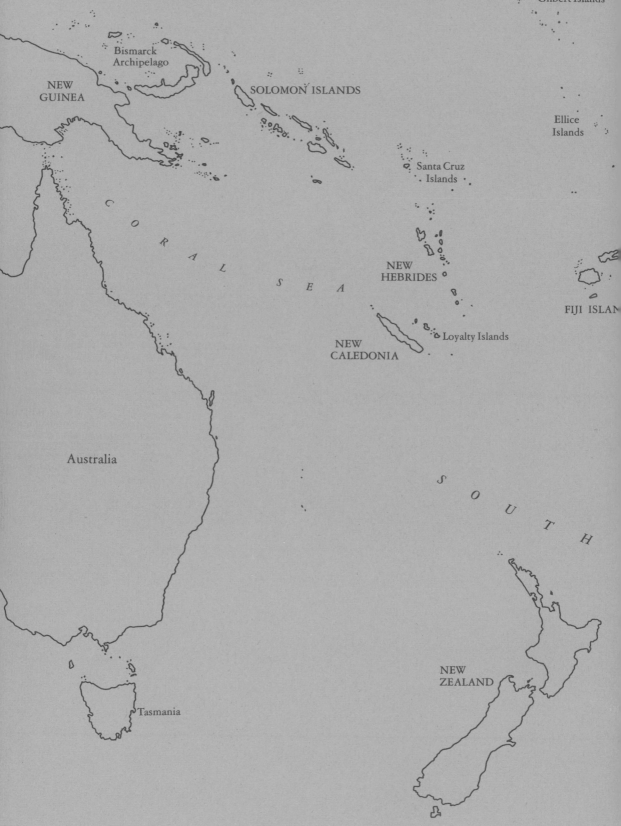